Answers to Prayer

Books by
Charles G. Finney
FROM BETHANY HOUSE PUBLISHERS

Answers to Prayer[3]
Autobiography of Charles G. Finney[1]
Finney on Revival[2]
Finney's Systematic Theology
Lectures on Revival
Principles of Prayer[3]

[1]Condensed and edited by Helen Wessel
[2]Condensed and edited by V. Raymond Edman
[3]Compiled and edited by Louis G. Parkhurst, Jr.

CHARLES G. FINNEY

Answers to Prayer

Compiled and Edited by Louis Gifford Parkhurst, Jr.

BETHANYHOUSE

Minneapolis, Minnesota

Answers to Prayer
by Charles G. Finney
Compiled & edited by Louis Gifford Parkhurst, Jr.
Copyright © 1983, 2002

Newly updated, 2002

Cover design by Eric Walljasper

Published by Bethany House Publishers
A Ministry of Bethany Fellowship International
11400 Hampshire Avenue South
Bloomington, Minnesota 55438
www.bethanyhouse.com

Printed in the United States of America by
Bethany Press International, Bloomington, Minnesota 55438

Library of Congress Cataloging-in-Publication Data

Finney, Charles Grandison, 1792-1875.
    Answers to prayer : a remarkable prayer journey from one of America's
greatest evangelists / by Charles G. Finney ; compiled & edited by Louis Gifford
Parkhurst, Jr.
        p. cm.
    ISBN 0-7642-2594-4
    1. Prayer—Christianity. I. Parkhurst, Louis Gifford, 1946- II. Title.
    BV210.3 .F56   2002
    248.3'2—dc21   2002002714

To

My Parents

Who First Taught Me How to Pray

CHARLES G. FINNEY was one of America's foremost evangelists. Over half a million people were converted under his ministry in an age that offered neither amplifiers nor mass communications as tools. Harvard Professor Perry Miller affirmed the fact that "Finney led America out of the eighteenth century." As a theologian, he is best known for his *Revival Lectures* and his *Systematic Theology*.

LOUIS GIFFORD PARKHURST, JR., is pastor of the Stonegate Cumberland Presbyterian Church in Edmond, Oklahoma. He garnered a B.A., an M.A., and an M.L.I.S. from the University of Oklahoma and an M.Div. degree from Princeton Theological Seminary. He has published more than thirty books in English and other languages, including the Finney Principles series with Bethany House. Since 1989, he has written more than six hundred weekly Bible lessons for *The Daily Oklahoman*. He is married and the father of two children.

Contents

Introduction

Answers to Prayer is the companion volume to Charles G. Finney's *Principles of Prayer*, and it has been prompted by the keen interest shown in the remarkable experiences of answered prayer in his life. During my lectures on Finney's *Principles of Prayer*, people have indicated further interest in how these principles were applied by Finney in his life and ministry. Finney discovered his principles of prayer by studying the Scriptures prayerfully, by enlightenment from the Holy Spirit, and by experiencing amazing answers to prayer.

I have carefully explored the previously unpublished version of Finney's *Autobiography* and from that have included previously omitted material (within brackets in the text). Some of this new material is quite startling and informative. The very interesting material on Finney's prayer life in Appendix A is from Finney's biography, written by his close friend and associate at Oberlin College, Professor G. Frederick Wright.

To help you apply what Finney discovered about prayer, I have begun each autobiographical sketch with an appropriate quotation from *Principles of Prayer*. At the conclusion of each sketch, I have asked a question to encourage you to probe more deeply into what you have just read, and to possibly stimulate prayer group discussion. Each question, along with the autobiographical sketch, should drive us to prayer and to renew our commitment to Christ and His Great Commission. Each of these sketches on answered prayer contains one or more important principle that we need to recognize, relate to, and apply to our lives. These would aid in prayer group discussion, confession, and revival if studied prior to each meeting by each member. My personal prayer is that this book will motivate each person to pray and to seek the help of the Holy Spirit in his walk and witness.

I wish to give special thanks to the late Gordon C. Olson of Bible Research Fellowship for providing me with his personal copy of Finney's *Autobiography* as the basis for the new materials in this book. Gordon Olson spent over one hundred and fifty hours making a page-by-page comparison of the 1876 edition with the secretarial handwritten "Memoirs in Manuscript" of over one thousand pages in the Oberlin College Library. His personal copy of the *Autobiography* contains all the important variations and additions, and the copied and typed sheets are pasted into his printed volume in their proper place. I am also grateful to him for the Testimonial Letter in Appendix B, which I was happy to discover while doing research in Olson's fine collection of materials on Charles Finney.

For the sake of His kingdom,
L. G. Parkhurst, Jr.

Chapter 1

First Prayer Meetings

Prevailing or effectual prayer is the prayer that attains the
blessing it seeks. It is the prayer that effectually moves God. The
very idea of effectual prayer is that it affects its object.[1]

In the church I attended, I was particularly struck by the fact that the
prayers I had listened to from week to week were not, that I could see,
being answered. In fact, I understood from the group's utterances in
prayer and from other remarks in their meetings that those who
offered them did not regard them as answered either.

When I read my Bible, I learned what Christ said in regard to
prayer and answers to prayer: "Ask and it will be given to you; seek
and you will find; knock and the door will be opened to you. For
everyone who asks receives; he who seeks finds; and to him who
knocks, the door will be opened" (Matthew 7:7–8). I read also what
Christ affirms: that God is more willing to give His Holy Spirit to
them that ask Him than earthly parents are to give good gifts to their
children. I heard them pray continually for the outpouring of the Holy
Spirit, and also as often confess that they did not receive what they
asked for.

---

[1]Charles G. Finney; L. G. Parkhurst, Jr., editor, *Principles of Prayer* (Minneapolis: Bethany House, 2001), 17.

They exhorted each other to a more active witness and to pray earnestly for revival, asserting that if they did their duty, prayed for the outpouring of the Holy Spirit, and were in earnest, the Spirit of God would be poured out; they would have a revival, and non-Christians would be converted. But in their prayer and conference meetings they would continually confess that they were making no progress in securing revival.

This inconsistency, the fact that they prayed so much and were not answered, was a hindrance to my own conversion. I did not know what to make of it. It was a question in my mind whether these persons were truly Christians, and whether they truly prevailed with God; or did I misunderstand the promises and teachings of the Bible on this subject, or was I to conclude that the Bible was not true? Here was something inexplicable to me; and it seemed that it would almost drive me into skepticism. The teachings of the Bible did not correspond with the facts before my eyes.

On one occasion when I was in one of the prayer meetings, I was asked if I wanted them to pray for me. I told them no, because I did not see that God answered their prayers. I said, "I suppose I need to be prayed for, for I know I am a sinner; but I do not see that it will do any good for you to pray for me, for you are continually asking but you do not receive. You have been praying for revival ever since I have been in Adams [New York], and yet you do not have it. You have been praying for the Holy Spirit to descend upon you, and yet complain of your leanness." I recollect having used this expression at that time: "You have prayed enough since I have attended these meetings to have prayed the devil out of Adams, if there is any virtue in your prayers. But here you are praying on, and still complaining." I was quite serious in what I said, and a little irritable, I think, in consequence of my being brought so continually face to face with the truth, which was a new experience for me.

But on further reading of my Bible, it struck me that the reason their prayers were not answered was because they did not comply with the revealed conditions upon which God had promised to answer prayer. They did not pray in faith in the sense of expecting God to give them the things they asked for.

I thought about this for some time without being able to put it into words. However, this relieved me so far as questions about the truth of the gospel were concerned, and after struggling over it for some time, my mind became quite settled that whatever unanswered questions there might be either in my own mind or in my pastor's mind or in the mind of the church, the Bible was, nevertheless, the true Word of God.

This being settled, I was brought face to face with the question of whether I would accept Christ as presented in the gospel or pursue my own plans and goals. At this point, my mind was so deeply convicted by the Holy Spirit that I could no longer leave this question unsettled; nor could I long hesitate between the two courses of life presented to me.[2]

Question for Thought and Prayer

Does my prayer life and the prayer life of my church demonstrate the reality of God and answered prayer, or do we leave the impression that prayer doesn't really do any good?

---

[2]"Autobiography," 9–11. From *Memoirs of Rev. Charles G. Finney* (New York: A. S. Barnes & Company, 1876); henceforth, *Autobiography*.

Chapter 2

Conversion

It is the Holy Spirit who leads Christians to understand and
apply the promises of Scripture. . . . So it has been with many a
Christian: while deeply engaged in prayer he has seen passages of
Scripture he never thought of before as having such
appropriate application.[1]

The whole question of gospel salvation became clear to me in a manner most marvelous to me at the time. I think I saw then as clearly as
I ever have in my life the reality and fullness of the atonement of
Christ. I saw that His work was a finished work, and that instead of
having or needing any righteousness of my own to recommend me to
God, I had to submit myself to the righteousness of God through
Christ. Gospel salvation seemed to me to be an offer of something to
be accepted, that it was full and complete, and that all that was necessary on my part was to be willing to give up my sins and to accept
Christ. Salvation, it seemed to me, instead of being a thing to be
accomplished by my own works, was a thing to be found entirely in
the Lord Jesus Christ, who presented himself before me as my God
and my Savior.

But after this distinct revelation had remained for a very short

---

[1]*Principles of Prayer*, 64.

time in my mind, the question came clearly: "Will you accept it now, today?" I replied, "Yes, I will accept it today, or I will die in the attempt."

North of the village and over a hill laid a stretch of woods in which I was almost daily in the habit of walking when the weather was pleasant. It was now October, and the time was past for my frequent walks there. Nevertheless, instead of going to the office, I turned and directed my course toward the woods, feeling that I must be alone and away from all human contact so that I could pour out my prayer to God.

But still my pride was evident. As I crested the hill, it occurred to me that someone might see me and suppose that I was going away to pray, although there was not a person on earth that would have suspected such a thing had he seen me. But so great was my pride, and so possessed was I with the fear of man, that I remember creeping low along the fence until I got so far out of sight that no one from the village could see me. I then entered the woods about a quarter of a mile and found a place where some large trees had fallen across each other, leaving an open place between. There I saw I could make a kind of closet. I crept into this place and knelt down for prayer. As I entered the woods, I remember having said, "I will give my heart to God, or I never will come out of here." I repeated this again.

But when I attempted to pray, I found that my heart would not pray. I had supposed that if I could only be where I could speak aloud without being overheard, I could pray freely. But when I tried, I could not speak; that is, I had nothing to say to God; or at least I could say only a few words, and those were without heart. In my attempt to pray, I could hear a rustling in the leaves and would stop and look up to see if someone was coming. I did this several times.

Finally, almost in despair, I said to myself, "I cannot pray. My heart is dead to God and I cannot pray." Then I reprimanded myself for having promised to give my heart to God. [I thought I had made a rash promise that I would be obliged to break.][2] My inward soul hung back, and there was no reaching out of my heart to God. I began to feel deeply that it was too late; that God must have given up on me and I was past hope.

The thought occurred to me that my promise was too rash—that I would give my heart to God that day or die in the attempt. It seemed the promise was binding upon my soul, and yet I was going to break my vow. A great wave of depression and discouragement came over me, and I felt almost too weak to remain on my knees.

Just at that moment I again thought I heard someone approach and opened my eyes to see whether it were true. But right there the revelation of my pride as the great difficulty that stood in the way was distinctly shown to me. An overwhelming sense of my wickedness in being ashamed to have a human being see me on my knees before God took such possession of me that I cried at the top of my voice and exclaimed that I would not leave that place if all the men on earth and all the demons in hell surrounded me. "What!" I said, "such a degraded sinner as I am, on my knees confessing my sins to the great and holy God; and ashamed to have any human being, and a sinner like myself, find me on my knees endeavoring to make my peace with my offended God!" The sin appeared infinitely great. It completely humbled me before the Lord.[3]

At this point a passage of Scripture seemed to come into my mind with a flood of light: "Then you will call upon me and come and pray to me, and I will listen to you. You will seek me and find me when you seek me with all your heart" (Jeremiah 29:12–13). I instantly took hold of this with my whole heart. I had intellectually believed the Bible before, but never had the truth been so clear that faith was a voluntary

[2]All portions of this book within brackets have been added from the unpublished, unedited version of Finney's *Autobiography*.

[3]Finney discovered that pride was one of the chief obstacles to conversion. His use of the "anxious seat" was designed in part to deal with this particular sin.

trust instead of an intellectual state. I was as conscious of trusting at that moment in God's veracity as I was for my existence. Somehow I knew it was a passage of Scripture, although I do not think I had ever read it. I knew that it was God's Word, and God's voice, as it were, that spoke to me. I cried to Him, "Lord, I take you at your word. You know that I have searched for you with all my heart, and that I have come here to pray to you, and you have promised to hear me."

That seemed to settle the question that I could then, that day, perform my vow. The Spirit seemed to lay stress upon that idea in the text, "When you seek me with all your heart" (Jeremiah 29:13). The question of when, that is, of the present time, seemed to fall heavily on my heart. I told the Lord that I would take Him at His word; that He could not lie; and that I was sure He heard my prayer, and that He would be found of me.

He then gave me many other promises, both from the Old and the New Testaments, especially some most precious promises relating to our Lord Jesus Christ. I never can, in words, make any human being understand how precious and true those promises appeared to me. I took them one after the other as infallible truth, the assertions of God, who could not lie. They did not seem so much to fall into my intellect as into my heart, to be put within the grasp of the voluntary powers of my mind; and I seized hold of them, appropriated them, and fastened upon them with the grasp of a drowning man.

I continued thus to pray and to receive and appropriate promises for a long time—how long, I do not know. I prayed till my mind became so full that before I was aware of it, I was on my feet and almost running up the ascent toward the road. The question of my being converted had not so much as arisen to my thought; but as I went up, brushing through the leaves and bushes, I remember saying with great emphasis, "If I am ever converted, I will preach the Gospel."

I soon reached the road that led to the village and began to reflect upon what had happened; and I found that my mind had become most wonderfully quiet and peaceful. I said to myself, "What is this? I must have grieved the Holy Spirit entirely away. I have lost all my conviction. I'm no longer concerned about my soul. It must be that the Spirit has left me." "Why!" I thought, "I never was so far from being concerned about my own salvation in my life."[4]

Then I remembered what I had said to God while on my knees— that I would take Him at His word; and indeed I remembered a good many things I had said, and concluded that it was no wonder the Spirit of God had left me; that for such a sinner as I was to take hold of God's Word in that way was presumptuous if not blasphemous. I concluded that in my excitement I had grieved the Holy Spirit, and perhaps committed the unpardonable sin.[5]

I walked quietly toward the village; and so perfectly quiet was my mind that it seemed as if all nature listened. It was on the tenth of October, and a very pleasant day. I had gone into the woods immediately after an early breakfast, and when I returned to the village, I found it was dinnertime. Yet I had been wholly unconscious of the time that had passed; it appeared to me that I had been gone from the village only a short time.

But how was I to account for the peace of mind? I tried to recall my convictions to get back again the load of sin under which I had been laboring. But all sense of sin, all consciousness of present sin or guilt, had departed from me. I said to myself, "What is this, that I cannot arouse any sense of guilt in my soul, as great a sinner as I am?" I tried in vain to make myself anxious about my present state. I was

[4]One of Finney's best sermons describes how to reach this state of the converted man. It is found in Charles Finney; L. G. Parkhurst, Jr., editor, "Religion of the Law and the Gospel," *Principles of Victory* (Minneapolis: Bethany House, 1981), 137–45.

[5]Finney later discovered and advised such a bold use of the promises of the Scriptures on the part of the Christian: "You have Bibles. Search through them, and whenever you find a promise that you can use, fasten it in your mind before you go on. You will not get through the Book without discovering that God's promises mean just what they say," "How to Pray a Prayer of Faith," *Principles of Prayer*, 56.

so quiet and peaceful that I tried to feel concerned about that, lest it should be a result of my having grieved the Spirit away. But look at it any way I would, I could not be anxious at all about my soul or about my spiritual condition. The peace of mind was unspeakably great. I never could describe it in words. [No view that I could take and no effort that I could make brought back a sense of guilt or the least concern about my ultimate salvation.] The thought of God was sweet to my mind, and the most profound spiritual tranquility had taken full possession of me. This was a great mystery; but it did not distress or perplex me.[6]

Question for Thought and Prayer

Does my prayer life and my obedience to God's Word demonstrate that I believe the Bible to be truly God's Word; and do I claim His promises for the totality of my life and my walk in the Holy Spirit?

---

[6]*Autobiography*, 14–18.

Chapter 3

Meeting Jesus

A true Christian is active, but his activity and energy arise out of
a deep identification with the indwelling Spirit of Christ.
Christ is formed within him; the Spirit of Christ is the
energizing power of his soul.[1]

Just before evening of the day I gave my heart to Christ, the thought
took possession of my mind that as soon as I was left alone in the new
office, I would try to pray again, that I was not going to abandon my
newfound faith at any rate; and therefore, although I no longer had
any concern about my soul, still I would continue to pray.

By evening we got the books and furniture adjusted in the new
offices, and I made up a good fire in the open fireplace, hoping to
spend the evening alone. Just at dark, Squire Wright, seeing that everything was in order, said good-night and retired to his home. I had
accompanied him to the door, and as I closed it and turned around,
my heart seemed to melt within me. All my emotions seemed to rise
and flow out, and the cry of my heart was, "I want to pour my whole
soul out to God." The rising of my soul was so great that I rushed into
the [counsel] room back of the front office to pray.

There was no fire and no light in the room; nevertheless, it

---

[1]*Principles of Prayer*, 103.

appeared to me as if it were perfectly light. As I went in and shut the door after me, it seemed as if I met the Lord Jesus Christ face to face. It did not occur to me then, nor did it for some time afterward, that it was wholly a mental image. On the contrary, it seemed to me that [I met Him face to face] as I would any other man. He said nothing, but looked at me in such a manner as to humble me at His feet. I have always since regarded this as a most remarkable experience, for it seemed to me a reality that He stood before me, and I fell down at His feet and poured out my soul to Him. I wept aloud like a child and made such confessions as I could with my choked utterance. It seemed to me that I bathed His feet with my tears, and yet I had no distinct impression that I touched Him.

I must have continued in this state for a good while; but my mind was too much absorbed with the interview to remember anything that I said. But I know that as soon as my mind became calm enough to break off the dialogue, I returned to the front office and found that the fire I had made of large wood was nearly burned out. But as I turned and was about to take a seat by the fire, I received a mighty baptism of the Holy Spirit. Without any expectation of it, without ever realizing there was any such thing for me, without any recollection that I had ever heard of the experience mentioned by any person in the world [at a moment entirely unexpected by me], the Holy Spirit descended upon me in a manner that seemed to go through me, body and soul. I could feel the impression like a wave of electricity going through and through me. Indeed, it seemed to come in waves and waves of liquid love, for I cannot express it in any other way. [And yet it did not seem like water but rather like the breath of God.] I remember distinctly that it seemed to fan me, like immense wings; [and it seemed to me, as these waves passed over me, that they literally moved my hair like a passing breeze].

No words can convey the wonderful love that was shed abroad in my heart. [It seemed to me that I would burst.] I wept aloud with joy and love, and I do not know but that I literally shouted out the unutterable yearnings of my heart. These waves came over me and over me, one after the other, until I cried out, "I shall die if these waves continue to pass over me!" I said [to the Lord], "Lord, I cannot bear any more," yet I had no fear of death.

How long this baptism continued to roll over me and go through me, I do not know. But it was late in the evening when a member of the church, a choir member—for I was the leader of the choir—came into the office to see me. He found me in this state of loud weeping, and said to me, "Mr. Finney, is something wrong?" I could give him no answer for some time. He then said, "Are you in pain?" I gathered myself up as best I could and replied, "No, but so happy that I cannot live."[2]

Question for Thought and Prayer

Have I so surrendered my life to the Lord Jesus Christ that I know the reality of His presence in my life?

---

[2]*Autobiography*, 19–21.

Chapter 4

Justified by Faith

The Holy Spirit was sent into the world by the Savior to guide
His people, to instruct them, and to bring things to their
remembrance, as well as to convince the world of sin.[1]

When I awoke in the morning, the sun had risen and was pouring
clear light into my room. I cannot tell you the impression this sunlight
made upon me. Instantly the baptism I had received the night before
returned upon me in the same manner. I arose upon my knees in the
bed and wept aloud with joy, and remained for some time too much
overwhelmed with the baptism of the Spirit to do anything but pour
out my soul to God. It seemed as if this morning's baptism was
accompanied with a gentle reproof, and the Spirit seemed to say to
me, "Will you doubt? Will you doubt?" I cried, "No! I will not doubt;
I cannot doubt." He then cleared the subject up so much in my mind
that it was, in fact, impossible for me to doubt that the Spirit of God
had taken possession of my soul.

In this state I was taught the doctrine of justification by faith as a
present experience. The doctrine had never taken such possession of
my mind that I ever viewed it as a fundamental doctrine of the gospel.
Indeed, I did not know what it meant in the proper sense. But I could

[1]*Principles of Prayer*, 65.

now see and understand what was meant by the passage: "Since we have been justified through faith, we have peace with God through our Lord Jesus Christ" (Romans 5:1). I could see that the moment I believed while up in the woods, all sense of condemnation had entirely left me, and that from that moment I could not feel a sense of guilt or condemnation by any effort whatsoever. My sense of guilt was gone; my sins were gone; and I do not think I felt any more sense of guilt than I would have had I never sinned.

This was the revelation I needed. I felt justified by faith; and so far as I could see, I was in a state in which I simply did not sin. Instead of feeling that I was sinning all the time, my heart was so full of love that it overflowed. My cup ran over with blessing and love, and I did not feel that I was sinning against God. Nor could I recover the least sense of guilt for my past sins. I said nothing of this experience to anyone at the time, as I recall; that is, of the experience of justification [and so far as I could see, of present sanctification].[2]

---

[2]*Autobiography*, 22–23. A comprehensive definition of justification and sanctification is found in *Finney's Systematic Theology* (Minneapolis: Bethany House, 1994). The following summary is taken from that book:

The disinterested and infinite love of God, the Father, Son, and Holy Spirit, is the true and only foundation of the justification and salvation of sinners. . . . A sanctifying faith unites the believer to Christ as his justification; but be it always remembered that no faith receives Christ as a justification that does not receive Him as a sanctification to reign within the heart. . . . To sanctify oneself is voluntarily to set oneself apart, to consecrate oneself to God. . . . Nothing is acceptable to God as a condition of justification and of consequent salvation, but a repentance that implies a return to full obedience to the moral law. . . . This obedience is not rendered independent of the grace of God, but is induced by the indwelling Spirit of Christ received by faith and reigning in the heart. . . . Justification . . . consists not in the law pronouncing the sinner just, but in his being ultimately, governmentally treated as if he were just; that is, it consists in a governmental decree of pardon or amnesty . . . upon the conditions of atonement, repentance, faith . . . present sanctification, in the sense of present full consecration to God . . . and perseverance in faith and obedience" (chapters 25–26, "Justification" and "Sanctification." See especially pages 361–62 for a succinct summary of justification).

Question for Thought and Prayer

Can I approach God in my prayers, knowing that I have been cleansed from all my sins by the shed blood of His Son, and can I claim this as a present experience, knowing that if I confess my sins He is faithful and just to forgive me of all my sins and cleanse me of all unrighteousness?[3]

---

[3]Finney wrote in his *Principles of Prayer:* "Confess and forsake your sins. God will never lead you as one of His own and share with you His secrets unless you confess and forsake sin," 76.

His First Conversions

If your feelings are truly benevolent, consider that it is the
Holy Spirit leading you to pray for things
according to the will of God.[1]

I spoke with many persons that day, and I believe the Spirit of God made lasting impressions upon every one of them.[2] I cannot remember one whom I spoke with who was not soon afterward converted. That evening I called at the home of a friend where a young man lived who was employed in distilling whiskey. The family had heard that I had become a Christian, and as they were about to sit down to tea, they urged me to sit down and take tea with them. The man of the house and his wife were both professing Christians. But a sister of the woman, who was present, was an unconverted young girl; and the young man of whom I spoke, a distant relative of the family, was a professed Universalist.

I sat down with them to tea, and they requested that I ask a blessing. Though I had never prayed like this before, I did not hesitate a moment but commenced to ask the blessing of God as we sat around the table. I had scarcely begun before the condition of these young

---

[1]*Principles of Prayer*, 71.
[2]This was the *first* day after Finney's conversion.

people came before my mind. I felt such compassion for them that I burst into weeping and was unable to proceed. Everyone around the table sat speechless for a short time, while I continued to weep. Directly, the young man moved back from the table and rushed out of the room. He fled to his bedroom and locked the door, and was not seen again until the next morning when he came out thoroughly converted to Christ. He has been for many years an able minister of the gospel.

That evening without any announcement having been made that I knew of, I noticed that people were going to the place where they usually held their conference and prayer meetings. My conversion had created quite a stir in the village. I later learned that some time before this some members of the church had proposed in a church meeting to make me a particular subject of prayer, and that Mr. Gale, the minister, had discouraged them, saying that he did not believe I would ever be converted, that from conversing with me he had found that I was very much informed upon the subject of Christianity and very much hardened.[3] And furthermore, he said he was discouraged that I led the choir and taught the young people sacred music, because they were so much under my influence that he did not believe they would ever be converted while I remained in Adams.

However, with one word the people seemed to rush to the place of worship; I went there myself. The minister was there together with nearly all the important people in the village. No one seemed ready to open the meeting, but the house was packed to capacity. I did not wait for anyone, but stood up and began by saying that I knew Christianity was true. I went on by telling the parts of my experience that seemed important to tell.

As soon as I finished speaking, Mr. Gale, the minister, stood and made a confession. He said he believed he had stood in the way of the

---

[3]Mr. Gale, a graduate of Princeton Theological Seminary, was the minister of the church Finney attended.

church, and then confessed that he had discouraged them when they proposed to pray for me. He also said that when he heard I was converted, he had promptly said he did not believe it. He said he had no faith for it. He spoke in a very humble manner.

I had never said a complete prayer in public. But soon after Mr. Gale was through speaking, he called on me to pray. I did so, and had a good deal of liberty. We had a wonderful meeting that evening, and from that day we had a meeting every evening for a long time.

As I had been a leader among the young people, I immediately called a meeting for them, which they all attended; that is, all with whom I was acquainted. I gave up my extra time to labor for their conversion, and the Lord blessed every effort that was made in a very wonderful manner. They were converted one after another with great rapidity, and the work continued among them until only one of their number was left unconverted.

After a short time, I went down to Henderson, where my father lived, and visited him. He was an unconverted man, and only one of my family—my youngest brother—had ever made a profession of Christ. My father met me at the gate and said, "How do you do, Charles?" I replied, "I am well, Father, body and soul. But, Father, you are an old man; all your children are grown up and have left your house; and I never heard a prayer in our home." My father dropped his head and burst into tears, and replied, "I know, Charles; come in and pray for us."

We went in, and I began to pray. My father and mother were greatly moved, and in a very short time thereafter they were both, I believe, converted. My mother may have had a secret hope before; but if she did, none of the family ever knew it.[4]

---

[4]*Autobiography*, 26–30.

Questions for Thought and Prayer

Since my own conversion and total commitment to Christ and His service, have I labored in prayer and in sharing the truth of the gospel with those who do not know Christ but who are closest to me, those whom I have a great influence with because of our past relationships? Can I begin now to pray and to labor for the salvation of those I love who are nearest to me?

—Chapter 6—

Supernatural Light

He [the Holy Spirit] prays for us by stirring our senses. Not that
He immediately suggests to us words or guides our language,
but He enlightens our minds so that the truth takes hold of our
souls. He leads us to a deep consideration of the current issues
and the . . . result is deep feeling.[1]

Toward spring the older members of the church began to lose their
zeal. I had been in the habit of rising early in the morning and spending time in prayer alone in the meetinghouse. I finally succeeded in
interesting a considerable number of brethren to meet with me there
in the mornings for a prayer meeting. This was at a very early hour,
and we were generally together long before it was light enough to read.
I even persuaded my minister to attend these morning meetings. But
soon they all began to stop coming.

One morning I had made several calls on the brethren, and when
I returned to the meetinghouse only a few of them had gotten there.
Mr. Gale was standing at the door, and as I came up, all at once the
glory of God shone upon and around me in a manner most marvelous. The day was just beginning to dawn, and the light that shone in
my soul almost leveled me to the ground. In this light it seemed as if

---

[1]*Principles of Prayer*, 63.

I could see that all nature, except man, praised and worshiped God. This light seemed to be like the brightness of the sun in every direction. It was too intense for the eyes. I remember casting my eyes down and breaking into a flood of tears in view of the fact that mankind did not praise God. I think I knew something then by actual experience of the light that prostrated Paul on his way to Damascus. It was a light I could not have endured long.

When I burst into such weeping, Mr. Gale said, "What is the matter, brother Finney?" I could not tell him. I found that he had seen no light, and that he saw no reason why I should be in such a state of mind. I therefore said little. I believe I merely replied that I saw the glory of God and that I could not endure to think of the manner in which men treated Him. Indeed, it did not seem to me at the time that the vision of His glory was to be described in words. I wept some more, and the vision passed away and left my mind calm.

I used to have many seasons of communing with God that cannot be described in words. And many times those seasons would end in an impression on my mind like "See that you don't tell anyone" (Matthew 8:4). I did not understand this at the time, and several times I paid no attention to the injunction, but tried to tell my Christian brethren what communications the Lord had made to me or what kind of communion I had with Him. But I soon found that it was useless to tell anyone what was passing between the Lord and my soul. They could not understand it. They would look surprised and sometimes even incredulous. I soon learned to keep quiet in regard to those divine manifestations or to say little about them.

I used to spend a great deal of time in prayer, sometimes literally praying "without ceasing." I also found it profitable and felt very much inclined to hold frequent days of private fasting. On those days I would seek to be entirely alone with God.

Sometimes I would pursue a wrong course in fasting and attempt to examine myself according to the ideas of self-examination that were then entertained by my minister and the church. I would try to look into my own heart in an attempt to examine my feelings and would turn my attention particularly to my motives and the state of my mind. But when I pursued this course, I found invariably that the day would close without any perceptible advances being made. Afterward I saw clearly why this was so. Turning my attention as I did from the Lord Jesus Christ and looking into myself, examining my motives and feelings, my feelings all subsided. But whenever I fasted and let the Spirit take His own course with me, allowing Him to lead and instruct, I almost always found it useful. I discovered I could not live without enjoying the presence of God; and if at any time a cloud came over me, I could not rest, I could not study, I could not attend to anything with the least satisfaction or benefit until the air was again cleared between my soul and God.[2]

Questions for Thought and Prayer

Why do I seek a deeper and more personal relationship with God? Do I intend to tell others of my experiences? Am I always checking my spiritual pulse? Or do I seek to praise God and focus on Jesus that I might be empowered to know Him and witness for Him?

---

[2]*Autobiography*, 33–36.

Chapter 7

Assurance in Prayer

If we find by comparing our state of mind with the Bible that
we are led by the Spirit to pray for an individual, we have good
evidence to believe that God is prepared to bless that one.[1]

The Lord taught me in those early days of my Christian experience
many very important truths regarding the spirit of prayer. Not long
after I was converted, a woman in whose home I had boarded was
taken very sick. She was not a Christian, but her husband claimed to
be one. He came into our office one evening, being a brother of Squire
Wright, and said to me, "My wife will not live through the night." This
seemed to drive an arrow, as it were, into my heart. [I felt something
almost like a cramp seizing me in the region of my heart.] It came
upon me in the sense of a burden that crushed me [and a kind of
inward spasm], the nature of which I could not at all understand; but
with it came an intense desire to pray for that woman. The burden
was so great that I left the office almost immediately and went up to
the meetinghouse to pray for her. There I struggled but could not say
much. I could only groan with groanings as loud and deep [as would
have been impossible, I think, for me, had it not been for that terrible
pressure on my mind].

---

[1] *Principles of Prayer*, 67.

I stayed a considerable time in the church in this state of mind without relief. When I returned to the office I could not sit still. I could only pace the room and agonize. I returned to the meetinghouse again and went through the same process of struggling. For a long time I tried to make my prayer before the Lord, but somehow words could not express it. I could only groan and weep, without being able to say in words what I wanted to say. I returned to the office again and still found I was unable to rest. I returned a third time to the meetinghouse. At this time the Lord gave me power to prevail. I was enabled to roll the burden upon Him, and I obtained the assurance in my mind that the woman would not die now, and especially that she would never die in her sins.

I returned to the office. My mind was perfectly quiet, and I soon left and retired to rest. Early the next morning the husband came into the office smiling and said, "She's alive, and to all appearances better this morning." I replied, "She will not die with this sickness, you may rely on it. And she will never die in her sins." I do not know how I was made sure of this, but it was in some way very plain to me so that I had no doubt that she would recover. She did recover, and soon afterward she became a Christian.

At first I did not understand this exercise of mind that I passed through. But shortly after in relating it to a Christian brother, he said to me, "Why, that was the travail of your soul."[2] A few minutes' conversation and pointing me to certain Scriptures gave me to understand what it was.[3]

---

[2] Finney later wrote, "Do not deceive yourselves by thinking that you offer effectual prayer without this intense desire for a blessing. . . . Prayer is not effectual unless it is offered up with an agony of desire. The apostle Paul speaks of it as a travail of the soul," *Principles of Prayer*, 31.

[3] *Autobiography*, 36–37.

Questions for Thought and Prayer

For whom and for what things do I pray long and hard and often—for myself and for things that benefit me? Am I willing to commit myself to the Holy Spirit's leading to the point that I am willing to pray often and intensely for someone I hardly know?

Chapter 8

Patience in Prayer

You must persevere. You are not to pray for a thing once and
then cease, and call that the prayer of faith.[1]

I have spoken of one young woman belonging to the class of young
people of my acquaintance who remained unconverted. This attracted
a good deal of attention, and there was much conversation among
Christians about her case. She was naturally a charming girl and very
much informed on the subject of religion, but she remained unconverted.

One of the elders of the church and I agreed to make her a daily
subject of prayer, to continue to present her case to the Lord, morning, noon, and evening, until she was converted. I found myself greatly
burdened about her and more and more burdened as I continued to
pray for her. I soon found, however, that the elder who had entered
into this arrangement with me was losing prayerful concern for her.
But this did not discourage me. I continued to hold on relentlessly. I
also availed myself of every opportunity to converse plainly and
searchingly with her on the subject of her salvation.

After I had continued in this way for some time, one evening I
called on her at her home just as the sun was setting. As I came up to

---

[1] *Principles of Prayer*, 58.

the door, I heard a shriek and a scuffling inside. I stood and waited a bit before knocking. The woman of the house soon opened the door and held in her hand a portion of a book, which looked to be torn in two. She was pale and very agitated, and holding out half the book to me, said, "Mr. Finney, do you think my sister has become a Universalist?" The book was a defense of Universalism. She had discovered her sister reading it privately and had tried to get it away from her; it was the struggle over the book that I had heard when I arrived.

I received the information at the door, and I declined to go in. It struck me much the same way as the announcement that the sick woman was about to die; I became burdened down with great agony. As I returned to my room, some distance from the house, I felt almost as if I would collapse under the weight that was on my mind. I struggled and cried and agonized, but could not present the case before God in words, only in groans and tears.

It seemed to me that the discovery that the young woman instead of being converted was becoming a Universalist so astounded me that I could not break through with my faith and get hold of God in reference to her situation. There seemed to be a darkness hanging over the question, as if a cloud had risen up between God and me with regard to prevailing for her salvation.

However, I was obliged to retire that night without having prevailed. But as soon as it was light, I awoke, and the first thought I had was to beseech the God of grace again for that young woman. I immediately arose and fell upon my knees. No sooner was I there than the darkness gave way, and the whole subject opened to my mind; and as soon as I pled for her, God said to me, "Yes! yes!" *If He had spoken with an audible voice, it would not have been more distinctly understood than was this word spoken within my soul.* It instantly relieved all my anxiety. My mind became filled with the greatest peace and joy. I felt a complete certainty that her salvation was secure.

I was incorrect, however, regarding the timing, which was not particularly impressed upon my mind at the time of my prayer. I expected her to be converted immediately, but she was not. She remained in her sins for several months.[2]

Question for Thought and Prayer

Do I get discouraged and give up in witnessing and in praying for another's conversion if that one does not come to faith and repent of his or her sins on my timetable?

---

[2] *Autobiography*, 37–39.

Chapter 9

A Fateful Refusal

Prayer, to be effectual, must be by the intercession of the Spirit.
You can never expect to offer prayer according to
the will of God without the Spirit.[1]

Soon after I was converted, the man with whom I had been boarding for some time, who was a magistrate and one of the principal men in the place, having been elected a member of the legislature of the state, was deeply convicted of sin. I was praying daily for him and urging him to give his heart to God. His conviction became very deep; but still, from day to day he refused and did not become a Christian. My burden for him increased.

One afternoon several of his political friends had a protracted interview with him. On the evening of the same day, I attempted again to pray for him, as my concern for his conversion had become very great. In my prayer I had drawn very near to God. I do not remember ever to have been in more intimate communion with the Lord Jesus Christ than I was then. Indeed, His presence was so real that I was bathed in tears of joy and gratitude and love; and in this state of mind I attempted to pray for this friend. But the moment I did so, my mouth was shut. I found it impossible to pray a word for him. The

---

[1] *Principles of Prayer*, 30.

Lord seemed to say to me, "No! I will not hear it." An anguish seized upon me; I thought at first it was a temptation. But the door was shut in my face. It seemed as if the Lord said to me, "Speak no more to me of this matter." It pained me beyond words. I did not know what to make of it.

The next morning I saw him, and as soon as I brought up the question of submission to God, he said to me, "Mr. Finney, I will not discuss it until I return from the legislature. I stand committed to my political friends to carry out certain measures in the legislature that are incompatible with my first becoming a Christian. And I have promised that I will not discuss the subject until after I have returned from Albany."

From the moment of that exercise the evening before, I had no burden of prayer for him at all. And as soon as he told me what he had done, I understood it. I could see that his convictions were gone, and that the Spirit of God had left him. From that time he grew more careless and hardened than ever.

When the time arrived, he went to the legislature, and in the spring he returned an almost insane Universalist. I say almost insane because instead of having formed his opinions from any evidence or course of argument, he told me this: "I have come to this conclusion not because I have found it taught in the Bible, but because such a doctrine is so opposed to the carnal mind. It is a doctrine so generally rejected and spoken against as to prove that it is distasteful to the carnal or unconverted mind." This was astonishing to me. But everything else that I could get out of him was as wild and absurd as this. He remained in his sins, finally fell into moral decay, and died at last, as I have been told, a dilapidated man and in the full faith of his Universalism.[2]

---

[2]*Autobiography*, 39–41.

Question for Thought and Prayer

Do I really seek to know Christ in my prayers so as to know whom and what I can rightly pray for according to the leading of the Spirit of God?

── *Chapter 10* ──

Refusing Prayer and Choosing a Destiny

*If you are filled with the Spirit . . . you will be calm under
affliction . . . you will be resigned in death, always feel prepared
to die and not afraid to die, and you will be proportionately
more happy forever in heaven.*[1]

There was an old man in Evans Mills, who was not only a non-Christian but also very critical toward Christianity. He was very angry at the revival movement. I heard every day of his threatenings and blasphemies but chose to ignore it. He altogether refused to attend any meetings. But in the midst of his opposition, and when his anger was greatest, while sitting one morning at the table, he suddenly fell out of his chair with a stroke. A physician was immediately called, who, after a brief examination, told him that he would live but a very short time and that if he had anything to say, he must say it at once. He had just strength and time, as I was informed, to stammer out, "Don't let Finney pray over my corpse." This was the last of his opposition in that place.

During that revival my attention was called to a sick woman in

[1] *Principles of Prayer*, 96.

the community who had been a member of a Baptist church and was well known in the place, but people were unsure of her true spiritual condition. She was fast failing with tuberculosis and they begged me to call on her. I went and had a long conversation with her. She told me of a dream she had when she was a girl that made her think her sins were forgiven. She had settled all her hopes upon that dream, and no argument could convince her otherwise. I tried to persuade her that there was no evidence of her conversion in that dream. I told her plainly that her acquaintances affirmed that she had never lived a Christian life or held a Christian disposition; and I had come to try to persuade her to give up her false hope and see if she would not now accept Jesus Christ that she might be saved. I dealt with her as kindly as I could, and did not fail to make her understand what I meant. But she took great offense, and after I went away, complained that I tried to take away her hope and distress her mind. She died not long afterward. But her death has often reminded me of Dr. Nelson's book *The Cause and Cure of Infidelity*.[2] As this woman approached death, her eyes were opened, and before she left the world, she seemed to have such a glimpse of the character of God, of what heaven was, and of the holiness required to dwell there that she shrieked with agony and exclaimed that she was going to hell. In this state, I was informed, she died.

When still at Evans Mills, one afternoon a Christian brother called on me and asked me to visit his sister, who was fast failing with tuberculosis and was a Universalist. Her husband had led her into Universalism. The brother said he had not asked me to go to see her when her husband was at home, because he feared that he would be abusive, as he was determined that his wife should not be disturbed on the question of universal salvation. I went, and found her not at all at rest in her views of Universalism, and during my conversation with her

[2]David Nelson, *The Cause and Cure of Infidelity Including a Notice of the Author's Unbelief and the Means of His Rescue* (New York: American Tract Society, 1841).

she gave up these views entirely and appeared to embrace the gospel of Christ. I believe she held fast to this hope in Christ until she died.[3]

Question for Thought and Prayer

Am I willing to make the commitment in prayer and under the Holy Spirit's leading to discuss salvation with all that are in need of the gospel of Christ, regardless of their situation or nearness to death?

---

[3] *Autobiography*, 67–68.

Chapter 11

The Young People and Revival

The Holy Spirit gives to Christians a spiritual discernment
respecting the movements and developments of Providence. . . .
There is no doubt that a Christian may be made to discern
clearly the signs of the times so as to understand by Providence
what to expect and thus to pray for it in faith.[1]

In Adams, in the spring of the year, the older members of the church
began to greatly decline in their witness and zeal for God. This greatly
disturbed me, as it did the young converts. About this time I read a
newspaper article entitled "A Revival Revived." The substance of it was
that in a certain place there had been a revival during the winter, that
in the spring it declined, and that after earnest prayer was offered for
the continued outpouring of the Spirit, the revival was powerfully
revived. This article greatly burdened my heart.

I was at that time boarding with Mr. Gale, and I took the article
to him. I was so overcome with a sense of the divine goodness in
hearing and answering prayer, and with a felt assurance that He would
hear and answer prayer for the revival of His work in Adams, that I

---

[1]*Principles of Prayer*, 68.

went through the house weeping aloud like a child. Mr. Gale seemed surprised at my feelings and my expressed confidence that God would revive His work. The article made no such impression on him.

At the next meeting of the young people, I proposed that we observe a closet concert of prayer for the revival of God's work; that we should pray at sunrise, at noon, and at sunset in our private places of prayer, and continue this for one week, when we would come together again and see what more could be done. No other means would be used for the revival of God's work. But the spirit of prayer was immediately poured out wonderfully upon the young converts. Before the week was out I learned that some of them, when they would attempt to observe this time of prayer, would lose all their strength and be unable to rise to their feet or even kneel down in their prayer closets, and that some would lie prostrate on the floor and pray with unutterable groanings for the outpouring of the Spirit of God.

The Spirit was poured out, and before the week ended all the meetings were crowded and there was as much interest in spiritual things, I think, as there had been at any time during the revival.

And here, I am sorry to say, a mistake was made, or I should say, a sin committed, by some of the older members of the church, which resulted in a grieving of the Spirit of God. As I afterward learned, a considerable number of the older people resisted this new movement among the young converts. They were jealous of it. They did not know what to make of it, and felt that the young converts were out of place in being so forward and so urgent with the older members. This state of mind finally grieved the Spirit of God. [After I left Adams, the state of revival waned. Brother Gale was soon dismissed, being in poor health. He went away to Western, Oneida County, New York, to a farm to see if it would restore his health.] It was not long before alienations began to rise among the older members of the church, which finally resulted in a great backsliding in those who had allowed themselves to resist this latter revival.

The young people held out well. The converts, so far as I know, were almost universally sound and have been thoroughly efficient Christians.[2]

Question for Thought and Prayer

Have you so opened your life to God the Holy Spirit as to be able to see His providential working in life around you and in what some would simply call "chance happenings"?

---

[2]*Autobiography*, 44–45.

Chapter 12

God's School of Prayer

Entire consecration to God is indispensable to the prayer of
faith. You must live a holy life and consecrate all to God—your
time, talents, influence—all you have, all you are,
to be His entirely.[1]

The presbytery was finally called together at Adams to examine me;
and, if they could agree to do so, to license me to preach the Gospel.
This was in March 1824. . . . When they had examined me, they voted
unanimously to license me to preach.

At this meeting I first saw the Rev. Daniel Nash, a member of the
presbytery, who is generally known as "Father Nash." A large congregation was assembled to hear my examination. I got in a little late and
saw the man standing in the pulpit speaking to the people, as I supposed. He looked at me, I observed, as I came in, and was looking at
others as they passed up the aisles.

As soon as I reached my seat and listened, I realized that he was
praying. I was surprised to see him looking all over the house as if he
were talking to the people while, in fact, he was praying to God. Of
course, it did not sound to me much like a prayer, and he was at that
time in a very cold and backslidden state. . . .

---

[1] *Principles of Prayer*, 58.

Later, I again saw Father Nash at the meeting of the presbytery when I was licensed. After that he became ill with an inflammation in his eyes and for several weeks was shut away in a dark room. He could neither read nor write and, as I learned, gave himself up almost entirely to prayer. His own life was radically revived, and as soon as he was able to see, with a double black veil over his face, he departed on an evangelistic trip.

When he came to Evans Mills, he was full of the power of prayer. He was another man altogether from what he had been at any former period of his Christian life. I found that he had a prayer list of the names of persons whom he made subjects of prayer every day, and sometimes many times a day. Praying with him and hearing him pray in meetings, I found that his gift of prayer was wonderful and his faith almost miraculous.

There was a man in town who kept a tavern in a corner of the village, whose house was the resort of all the opposers of the revival. The barroom was a place of blasphemy, and he was himself a most profane, ungodly, abusive man. He went all over town mocking the revival and would take particular pains to swear and blaspheme whenever he saw a Christian.

Father Nash heard us speak of this man as "a hard case," and immediately put his name on his prayer list. He remained in town a day or two, and then went on his way, having in view another area.

Not many days afterward, as we were holding an evening meeting with a very crowded house, who should come in but this notorious tavern owner? His entrance created a considerable stir in the congregation. People feared that he had come in to make a disturbance. The fear and abhorrence of the man had become very general among Christians, so that when he came in, some of the people got up and left. I knew his countenance, and kept my eyes on him. I very soon became convinced that he had not come in to oppose but that he was under great conviction. He sat and writhed upon his seat and was very uneasy. He soon stood and trembling asked me if he might say a few words. I told him that he could. He then proceeded to make one of the most heartbreaking confessions that I have ever heard. His confession seemed to cover the whole ground of his treatment of God, of Christians, of the revival, and of everything good.

This thoroughly broke up the fallow ground in many hearts. It was the most powerful means that could have been used just then to give an impetus to the work. The man soon came out and began to witness, abolished all the revelry and profanity of his barroom, and from that time, as long as I stayed there, and beyond that I know not how much longer, a prayer meeting was held in his barroom nearly every night.[2]

Question for Thought and Prayer

Do I need to attend God's school of prayer, or am I now able to pray in faith from a consecrated heart for the salvation of those who seem farthest from God?

---

[2]*Autobiography*, 51–52, 70–72.

Chapter 13

Prayer for a New Heart

Sinners are not converted only by the direct contact of the Holy Spirit, but by the truth employed as a means. To expect the conversion of sinners by prayer alone, without the employment of truth, is to tempt God.[1]

The doctrines preached at Evans Mills were those that I always preached as the gospel of Christ. I insisted upon the voluntary total moral depravity of the unregenerate and the unalterable necessity of a radical change of heart by the Holy Spirit and by means of the truth.

I laid great stress upon prayer as an indispensable condition of promoting revival. The atonement of Jesus Christ, His divinity, His divine mission, His perfect life, His vicarious death, His resurrection; and repentance, faith, justification by faith, and all kindred doctrines, were discussed as thoroughly as I was able, and pressed home, and were manifestly made efficacious by the power of the Holy Spirit.

The means used were simply preaching, prayer and conference meetings, private prayer, personal conversation, and meetings for the instruction of serious inquirers. These and no other means were used for the promotion of the work.

I have spoken of the doctrines preached. I should add that I always

---

[1] *Principles of Prayer*, 19.

gave considerable instruction to inquirers. The practice had been, I believe, universal to set anxious sinners to praying for a new heart and to using means for their own conversion. The directions they received either assumed or implied that they were willing to become Christians and were asking God to convert them. I tried to make them understand that God was using the means with them and not they with Him; that God was willing, and they were unwilling; that God was ready, and they were not ready. In short, I tried to persuade them that present faith and repentance was what God required of them, present and instant submission to His will, present and instant acceptance of Christ. I tried to show them that delay was only an evasion of present duty; that praying for a new heart was trying to cast the responsibility of their conversion upon God; and that all efforts to do good works while they did not give their hearts to God were hypocritical and delusive.[2]

Question for Thought and Prayer
Have you willingly given your heart to God in faith and repentance, or are your prayers still self-seeking and concerned about what you think God needs to do in your heart to save you?

[2]*Autobiography*, 77, 79–80.

Chapter 14

Prayer and the Pulpit

✦ Truth, by itself, will never produce the effect without the Spirit of God, and the Spirit is given in answer to prayer.[1]

My habit has always been to study the gospel and the best applications of it all the time. I do not confine myself to hours and days of writing my sermons, but my mind is always pondering the truths of the gospel and the best ways of using them. I go among the people and learn their wants. Then, in the light of the Holy Spirit, I take a subject that I think will meet their present situation and necessities. I think intensely on it, and pray much over the subject on Sunday morning, for example, and fill my mind with it, and then go and pour it out to the people. Whereas, the great difficulty with a sermon that a man has written out is that he needs to think little on the subject. He needs to pray but a little. He perhaps reads over his manuscript Saturday evening or Sunday morning; but he does not feel the necessity of being powerfully anointed that his mouth may be opened and filled with arguments and that he may be enabled to preach out of a full heart. He is quite at ease. He has only to use his eyes and his voice, and he can preach in the way he is comfortable. It may be a sermon that has been written for years, or it may be a sermon that he has written

---

[1] *Principles of Prayer*, 18–19.

within the week. But on Sunday there is no freshness in it. It does not come necessarily new and fresh as an anointed message from God to his heart and through his heart to his people.

When I first began to preach, and for some twelve years of my earliest ministry, I did not write down a word, and was most commonly obliged to preach without any preparation whatsoever, except what I got in prayer. Often I went into the pulpit without knowing upon what text I should speak or a word that I should say. I depended on the occasion and on the Holy Spirit to suggest the text and to open up the whole subject to my mind; and certainly in no part of my ministry have I preached with greater success and power. If I did not preach from inspiration, I did not know how to preach. It was a common experience with me, and has been during all my ministerial life, that the subject would be opened up to my mind in a manner that was surprising to me. It seemed that I could see with intuitive clearness just what I ought to say; and whole platoons of thoughts, words, and illustrations came to me as fast as I could deliver them. When I first began to make sermon outlines, I made them after rather than before I preached. It was to preserve the outline of the thought that had been given me on occasions such as I have just mentioned. I found that when the Spirit of God gave me a very clear view of a subject, I could not retain it to be used on any other occasion unless I jotted down an outline of the thoughts. But after all, I have never found myself able to use old outlines in preaching, to any considerable extent, without rewriting them and having a fresh and new view of the subject given me by the Holy Spirit. I almost always get my subjects on my knees in prayer; and it has been a common experience with me, upon receiving a subject from the Holy Spirit, to have it make such a strong impression on my mind that I tremble, and it is difficult to write. When subjects are thus given me that seem to go through me, body and soul, I can in a few moments make an outline that will enable me to retain the view presented by the Spirit; and I find that such sermons always come with great power upon the people.

I am prepared to say, very seriously, that I think I have studied all the more for not having written my sermons. I have been obliged to make the subjects on which I preached familiar to my thoughts, to fill my mind with them, and then to go and give them to the people. I simply note the main points upon which I wish to dwell in the briefest possible manner and in language that I do not actually use in preaching. I simply jot down the order of my propositions, and the propositions that I propose to take; and in a word, sketch an outline of the remarks and inferences with which I conclude.[2]

Question for Thought and Prayer

In how much of my Christian ministry and service to others do I rely more upon my thoughts and actions than upon prayer and the work of the Spirit of God?

---

[2]*Autobiography*, 94–96.

Chapter 15

Prayer Conquers Fear

*If you have the Spirit of God you must expect to feel great
distress in view of the condition of the church and of the
world. . . . Read your Bibles and see how the prophets and
apostles were always distressed in view of the state
of the church and of the world.*[1]

It was on Friday, if I remember right, that I arrived at Antwerp. (The
people had no desire for public worship, and therefore the meetinghouse was locked up.) I called on some pious women and asked them
if they would like to have a meeting. They said that they would, but
they did not know that it would be possible. One woman agreed to
open her parlor that evening for a meeting if I could get anyone to
attend. I went about and invited the people, and secured the atten-
dance, I think, of some thirteen in her parlor. I preached to them and
then said that if I could get the use of the village schoolhouse, I would
preach on Sunday. I got the consent of the trustees, and the next day
an announcement was circulated around among the people for a
meeting at the schoolhouse Sunday morning.

In passing around the village I heard a vast amount of profanity. I
thought I had never heard so much in any place I ever visited. It

---

[1] *Principles of Prayer*, 88.

seemed as if the men, in playing ball on the green, and in every business place that I stepped into, were all cursing and swearing and damning each other. I felt as if I had arrived at the borders of hell. I had a kind of sickening feeling, I recall, as I milled about the village on Saturday. The very atmosphere seemed to me to be like a poison, and a kind of fear took possession of me.

I gave myself to prayer later on Saturday and urged my petition until this answer came: "Do not be afraid; keep on speaking, do not be silent. For I am with you, and no one is going to attack and harm you, because I have many people in this city" (Acts 18:9–10). This completely relieved me of all fear. I found out, however, that the Christian people there were actually afraid that something serious might happen if religious meetings were again established in that place. When circulating the village on Saturday, I also discovered that the announcement given about preaching at the schoolhouse was making quite a stir.

Sunday morning I arose early and left my lodgings in the hotel in order to get alone where I could lift up my voice as well as my heart. I went up into the woods and continued for a long time in prayer, but coming away without much relief of my burden, I went up a second time, only to have the load upon my mind increase. After a third trip, the answer came. And then it was time for the meeting, so I went immediately to the schoolhouse. I found it packed to capacity. I had my pocket Bible in my hand and read to them this text: "For God so loved the world that he gave his one and only Son, that whoever believes in him shall not perish but have eternal life" (John 3:16). I cannot remember much that I said, but I know that the point on which my mind principally labored was the treatment that God received in return for His love. The subject affected my own mind very much, and I preached and poured out my soul and my tears together.

I saw several of the men there from whom I had the day before heard the most awful profanity. I pointed them out in the meeting and told what they had said—how they had called on God to damn each other. Indeed, I let loose my whole heart upon them. I told them they seemed "to howl blasphemy about the streets like hell-hounds"; and it seemed to me that I had arrived "on the very verge of hell." Everyone knew what I said was true. They cowered under it. They did not appear offended, but the people wept about as much as I did. I think there were scarcely any dry eyes in the house.

The caretaker had refused to open the meetinghouse that morning, but as soon as these first services closed, he stood up and said to the people that he would open the meetinghouse in the afternoon.

The people scattered and carried the information in every direction, and in the afternoon the meetinghouse was almost as crowded as the schoolhouse had been in the morning. Everyone, it seemed, was out at meeting; and the Lord fell upon them in a convicting manner.[2]

Question for Thought and Prayer

Do I often not speak out because I am afraid of people and of what they might say and do, or do I consistently pray for the Spirit of God to give me courage and a promise from Scripture?

---

[2]*Autobiography*, 99–100.

Chapter 16

Prayer and Revival

These strong desires vividly illustrate the strength of God's feelings. They are like the real feelings of God for impenitent sinners. When I have seen, as I sometimes have, the amazing strength of love for souls that has been felt by Christians, I have been wonderfully impressed with the amazing love of God and His desire for their salvation.[1]

I have said that the spirit of prayer that prevailed in revivals was a very marked feature of them. It was common for young converts to be greatly burdened in prayer; and in some instances so much so that they were constrained to pray whole nights, until their bodily strength was quite exhausted, for the conversion of souls around them. There was a certain pressure of the Holy Spirit upon the minds of Christians, and they seemed to bear the burden of immortal souls. They manifested a serious frame of mind and watchfulness in all their words and actions. It was very common to find Christians, whenever they met anywhere, instead of engaging in conversation, to fall on their knees in prayer.

Not only were prayer meetings greatly multiplied and fully attended but there was a mighty spirit of private prayer as well. It was

[1] *Principles of Prayer*, 36.

often heard that two or more would take the promise "If two of you on earth agree about anything you ask for, it will be done for you by my Father in heaven" (Matthew 18:19) and make some particular person a subject of prayer; and it was wonderful to what an extent they prevailed. Answers to prayer were so manifestly multiplied on every side that no one could escape the conviction that God was daily and hourly answering prayer.

If anything occurred that threatened to mar the work, if there was any appearance of any root of bitterness springing up, or any tendency to fanaticism or disorder, Christians would sound the alarm and give themselves to prayer that God would direct and control all things. And it was surprising to see to what extent and by what means God would remove obstacles out of the way in answer to prayer.

In regard to my own experience, I will say that unless I had the spirit of prayer I could do nothing. If even for a day or an hour I lost the spirit of grace and supplication, I found myself unable to preach with power and efficiency or to win souls by personal conversation. In this respect my experience was what it has always been. [I found myself having more or less power in preaching and in personal labors for souls in proportion as I had the spirit of prevailing prayer. I have found that unless I kept myself and have been kept in such relationship to God as to have daily and hourly access to Him in prayer, my efforts to win souls were abortive; but that when I could prevail with God in prayer, I could prevail with men in preaching, exhortation, and conversation.]

[I have stated that my last field of labor in St. Lawrence County was in De Kalb, and that the revival there was powerful for the scattered populations that then existed in that new region of the country.] For several weeks before I left De Kalb to go to the synod [in Oneida County of which I have made mention], I was very strongly exercised in prayer and had an experience that was somewhat new to me. I found myself so agonized and so borne down with the weight of immortal souls that I was constrained to pray without ceasing. [I could not rest in the house and was obliged to retire to the barn frequently throughout the day, where I would unburden my soul and pour out my heart to God in prayer. I had wonderful faith given to me at that time, and had some experiences that alarmed me. When alone I would wrestle and struggle, and pray faith would rise until I would say to God] that He had made a promise to answer prayer, and I could not, and would not, be denied. [I could be so burdened as to use strong language with God in prayer.] I felt so certain that He would hear me, and that faithfulness to His promises and to himself rendered it impossible that He should not hear and answer, that frequently I found myself saying to Him, "I hope Thou dost not think that I can be denied. I come with Thy faithful promises in my hand, and I cannot be denied."

[At that time the Spirit of God made such application of the promises to my mind and so revealed their real meaning that I was led to understand better how to use them and to what cases they were especially applicable than I had ever understood before. I had been in the habit from the witness of my first conversion of having the Spirit in prayer lead me to such application of the promises as I never would have gotten by any study of my own. I had also come to realize that these promises had a much wider application in their spirit than a mere critical examination of their face value would have warranted. I was led frequently to see that the New Testament writers quoted the promises of the Old Testament in such a way as to cover much more ground than the mere letter of the promises would have implied. But this experience of mine at De Kalb was extraordinary in this respect.][2]

I cannot tell how absurd unbelief looked to me and how certain I was in my mind that God would answer prayer—those prayers that from day to day and from hour to hour I found myself offering in

---

[2]See Appendix A for G. P. Wright's comments on Finney's prayer of faith.

such agony and faith. I had no idea of the shape the answer would take, the locality in which the prayers would be answered, or the exact time of the answer. My impression was that the answer was near, even at the door; and I felt myself strengthened in the divine life, put on the harness for a mighty conflict with the powers of darkness, and expected soon to see a far more powerful outpouring of the Spirit of God in that new region where I had been laboring.[3]

Question for Thought and Prayer

Have I so studied God's Word, and am I so open to the Holy Spirit's guidance, that I can understand who and what I am to pray for and can apply the promises of Scripture to the needs I perceive?

[3]*Autobiography*, 141–43.

Chapter 17

Family Prayer

True religion does not consist in obeying our feelings but in
conforming our heart to the law of our intelligence. God
has given us reason, and requires us to understand
what we are about.[1]

I remember the situation of a young woman at Western, in a distant
part of the town, who came to the meeting at the center almost every
day. I had conversed with her several times and found her deeply convicted, and indeed, almost in despair. I was expecting to hear, from
day to day, that she had been converted; but she remained unchanged,
except that her despair increased. This led me to suspect that something was wrong at home. I asked her if her parents were Christians.
She said they were members of the church. I asked her if they attended
meetings. She said, "Yes, on Sundays." "Do your parents not attend
meetings at other times?" "No," was the reply. "Do you have family
prayers at home?" "No, sir," she said. "We used to have; but we have
not had family prayers for a long time." This revealed the problem to
me at once. I inquired when I could possibly find her father and
mother at home. She said almost any time, as they were seldom away
from home. Feeling that it was infinitely dangerous to leave this case

---

[1] *Principles of Prayer*, 103.

as it was, I went the next morning to visit the family.

This daughter was, I think, an only child; at any rate, she was the only child at home. I found her dejected and deep in despair. I said to her mother, "The Spirit of the Lord is striving with your daughter." "Yes," she said, "I don't doubt that He is." I asked her if she was praying for her. She gave me an answer that led me to understand that she did not know what it was to pray for her daughter. I inquired after her husband. She said that he was in the field at work. I asked her to call him in. He came, and as he came in, I said to him, "Do you see the state that your daughter is in?" He replied that he thought she felt very badly. "And are you concerned and praying for her?" His answer revealed the fact that if he was ever converted, he was a backslider now and had no influence with God whatsoever. "And," I said, "you do not have family prayers." "No, sir." "Now," I said, "I have seen your daughter, day after day, bowed down with conviction, and I believe the difficulty is here at home. You have shut up the kingdom of heaven against your daughter. You neither enter yourself, nor will you allow her to enter. Your unbelief and worldly-mindedness prevent the conversion of your daughter and will ruin your own soul. Now, you must repent. I do not intend to leave this house until you and your wife repent and step out of the way of your daughter's being converted. You must establish family prayer and build up the altar that has fallen down. Now, my dear sir, will you get down here on your knees, you and your wife, and engage in prayer? And will you promise that from this time on you will do your duty, set up your family altar, and return to God?"

I was so strong with them that they both began to weep. My faith was such that I did not trifle with them when I said that I would not leave the house until they repented and established their family altar. I felt that the work must be done, and done then. I got down upon my knees and began to pray, and they knelt down and wept beside me. I confessed for them as well as I could, and tried to lead them to

God and to prevail with God on their behalf. It was a moving scene. They both humbled themselves and confessed their sins, and before we rose from our knees the daughter was manifestly converted. She arose, rejoicing in Christ. Many answers to prayer and many scenes such as this presented themselves in this revival.[2]

Question for Thought and Prayer

Is there any stumbling block in your life and in the life of your family that is influencing someone to resist God's call?

---

[2]*Autobiography*, 151–52.

Chapter 18

Prayer and Faith

You must pray in faith. You must expect to obtain the things for which you ask. Do not look for an answer to prayer if you pray without any expectation of obtaining it. You are not to form such expectations without any reason for them. In the cases I have supposed, there is a reason for the expectation.[1]

I should say a few words in regard to the kind of prayer that prevailed at Rome at this time. I think it was on the Saturday that I came down from Western to exchange with Mr. Gillett that I met the church people in the afternoon in a prayer meeting in their house of worship. I endeavored to make them understand that God would immediately answer prayer provided they fulfilled the conditions upon which He had promised to answer, and especially if they believed in the sense of expecting Him to answer their requests. I observed that they were greatly interested in my remarks and their countenance manifested an intense desire to see an answer to their prayers. Near the close of the meeting I recall making this remark: "I really believe that if you will unite this afternoon in the prayer of faith to God for the immediate outpouring of His Spirit, you will receive an answer from heaven sooner than you would get a message from Albany by the quickest mail service that could be sent."

---

[1] *Principles of Prayer*, 34.

I said this with great emphasis, and I felt it; and I noticed that the people were surprised by my expression of earnestness and faith in respect to an immediate answer to prayer. The fact is I had so often seen this result in answer to prayer that I made the remark without any misgivings. Nothing was said by any of the members of the church at the time, but I learned after the work had begun that three or four members of the church had called at Mr. Gillett's study and felt so impressed with what had been said about speedy answers to prayer that they determined to take God at His word and see whether He would answer while they were yet speaking. One of them told me afterward that they had wonderful faith given them by the Spirit of God to pray for an immediate answer, and he added, "The answer did come quicker than we could have gotten an answer from Albany by the quickest mail service that could have been sent."

Indeed, the town was full of prayer. Go where you would, you heard the voice of prayer. Pass along the street, and if two or three Christians happened to be together, they were praying. Wherever they met they prayed. Wherever there was a sinner unconverted, especially if he manifested any opposition, you would find some two or three brethren or sisters agreeing to make him a particular subject of prayer; [and it was very remarkable to see to what an extent God would answer prayer immediately].[2]

Question for Thought and Prayer

Is your relationship with God so developed that you know what things to pray for in faith and know that to encourage others in specific prayers will increase their faith?

---

[2]*Autobiography*, 171–72.

Chapter 19

Prayer and Opposition

If you have much of the Spirit of God, you must make up your
mind to have much opposition both in the church and in the
world. Very likely the leading men in the church will oppose
you. So it was when Christ was on earth. . . . If you are filled
with the Spirit you will not find yourselves distressed, galled,
or worried when people speak against you.[1]

I must return to what happened at Auburn. I became, soon after I
went there, very impressed with the extensive working of that system
of espionage of which I have spoken.[2] Mr. Frost, of Whitesboro, had
come to a knowledge of the facts to a considerable extent and related
them to me. I said nothing publicly or, as I recall, privately, to anyone
on the subject but gave myself to prayer. I looked to God with great
earnestness day after day to be directed, asking Him to show me the
path of duty and to give me grace to ride out the storm.

I shall never forget the scene I passed through one day in my room
at Dr. Lansing's [in Auburn, soon after my arrival there]. The Lord
showed me as in a vision what [I had to pass through]. He drew so
near to me during prayer that my flesh literally trembled on my bones.

---

[1] *Principles of Prayer*, 90, 96.
[2] See the *Autobiography* for the complete details of this event.

I shook from head to foot [like a man in an epileptic seizure] under a full sense of the presence of God. At first, and for some time, it seemed more like being on top of Mount Sinai amid its full thundering than in the presence of the cross of Christ.

Never in my life that I can remember was I so awed and humbled before God as then. Nevertheless, instead of feeling like fleeing, I seemed drawn nearer and nearer to that presence that filled me with such unutterable awe and trembling. After a season of great humiliation before Him, there came a great lifting up. God assured me that He would be with me and uphold me; that no opposition would prevail against me; that I had nothing to do in regard to all this matter but to keep about my work and wait for the salvation of God.

I can never describe the sense of God's presence and all that passed between God and my soul at that time. It led me to be perfectly trustful, perfectly calm, and to have nothing but the most kind feelings toward all the brethren that were misled and were arraying themselves against me. I felt assured that all would come out right and that my true course was to leave everything to God and to keep about my work. And as the storm gathered and the opposition increased, I never for one moment doubted how it would end. I was never disturbed by it; I never spent a waking hour thinking of it, even when to all outward appearances it seemed as if all the churches of the land, except where I had labored, would unite to shut me out of their pulpits. This was indeed the avowed determination, as I understood, of the men who led the opposition. They were so deceived that they thought there was no effectual way but to unite and, as they expressed it, "put him down." But God assured me that they could not put me down.[3]

Question for Thought and Prayer

Can I pray to God for my enemies in the midst of their opposition to my work for Him, and do so with perfectly kind feelings toward those who are against me?

---

[3]*Autobiography*, 193–94.

Chapter 20

Prayer Overcomes Ignorance

*There are many who believe in the existence of God but
do not believe in the efficacy of prayer. They profess to believe
in God but deny the necessity or influence of prayer.*[1]

In the spring of 1829, when the Delaware River was high, the lumbermen came down with their rafts from the region of the high land, where they had been getting the lumber out during the winter. At that time there was a large tract of land along the northern region of Pennsylvania, called by many "the lumber region," that extended up toward the headwaters of the Delaware River.

Many of the lumbermen were raising families in that region, and this large piece of land was unsettled and unoccupied except by these lumbermen. They had no schools, and at that time no churches or religious privileges at all. I knew a minister who told me he was born in that lumber region and that at twenty years old he had never attended a religious meeting and did not know his alphabet.

The men that traveled down with lumber attended our meetings, and quite a number of them were converted. They went back into the

---

[1] *Principles of Prayer*, 44.

wilderness and began to pray for the outpouring of the Holy Spirit and to tell the people around them what they had seen in Philadelphia, exhorting them to attend to their salvation. Their efforts were immediately blessed, and the revival began to take hold and to spread among those lumbermen. It went on in a most powerful and remarkable manner. In fact, it spread to such an extent that in many cases persons would be convicted and converted who had not attended any meetings and who were almost as ignorant as heathen. Men who were working on getting the lumber out and were living in little shanties alone, or where two or three or more were together, would be seized with such conviction that it would lead them to wander off and inquire what they should do. They would be converted, and thus the revival spread. There was the greatest simplicity manifested by the converts.

An aged minister who had been somewhat acquainted with the circumstances related to me the following fact as an example of what was going on there. He said one man in a certain place had a little shanty by himself where he slept nights. He began to feel that he was a sinner and his convictions increased upon him until he broke down, confessed his sins, and repented; and the Spirit of God revealed to him so much of the way of salvation that he evidently knew the Savior. But he had never attended a prayer meeting or heard a prayer, as far as he knew, in his life. He finally got to the point where he felt constrained to go and tell some of his acquaintances how he felt. But when he arrived, he found that a good many of them felt just as he did and that they were holding prayer meetings. He attended their meetings and heard them pray and finally prayed himself, and this was the form of his prayer: "Lord, you have got me down and I hope you will keep me down. And since you have had such good luck with me, I hope you will try other sinners."

I have said that this work began in the spring of 1829 as the result of a few men having attended some of our meetings. In the spring of

1831 I was at Auburn again. Two or three men from this lumber region came to see me and to inquire how they could get some ministers to go in there. They said that not less than five thousand people had been converted in that region, that the revival had extended itself for eighty miles, and there was not a single minister of the gospel there.[2]

I have never been in that region personally, but from all I have ever heard about it, I have regarded that as one of the most remarkable revivals that have occurred in this country. It was carried on almost independently of the ministry among a class of people very ignorant in regard to all ordinary instruction, and yet so clear and wonderful were the teachings of God there that I have always understood that revival to be remarkably free from fanaticism, wildness, or anything objectionable. "Consider what a great forest is set on fire by a small spark" (James 3:5). The spark that was struck into the hearts of those few lumbermen that came to Philadelphia spread over that forest and resulted in the salvation of a multitude of souls.[3]

Questions for Thought and Prayer

Do I really understand how important my prayers and my witnessing are? The effort I expend today may lead thousands in other lands, or even those yet unborn, to find the Savior. Am I willing to expend that effort for the cause of God's kingdom?

---

[2]Let the reader not forget, however, that it was the preaching of Finney and the praying of Finney and others that motivated those few men to return with the gospel to their brothers in that region.

[3]*Autobiography*, 250–52. Finney, in his humility, does not underscore the great impact of the truth he preached upon the minds of those who declared that same truth to others in that region.

Chapter 21

Prayer and Difficult Decisions

There are three ways in which God's will is revealed to men for their guidance in prayer . . . by express promises or predictions in the Bible . . . by His providence . . . and by His Spirit.[1]

Leaving New York, I spent a few weeks in Whitestown, and as was common, being pressed to go in many directions, I was greatly at a loss as to what my duty was. But among others, an urgent invitation was received from the Third Presbyterian Church in Rochester, of which Mr. Parker had been pastor, to go there and supply them for a period of time.

I inquired into the circumstances and found that on several accounts it was a very unpromising field of labor.[2]

With many pressing invitations before me, I felt as I have often felt—greatly perplexed. I remained at my father-in-law's and considered the subject until I felt that I must take hold and work somewhere. Accordingly we packed our trunks and went down to Utica, about

---

[1] *Principles of Prayer*, 22.
[2] For details of the circumstances, see the *Autobiography*. Finney was always courageous in the Spirit, and did not flee difficult situations.

seven miles away, where I had many praying friends. We arrived there in the afternoon, and in the evening quite a number of the leading brethren in whose prayers and wisdom I had a great deal of confidence, at my request met for consultation and prayer in regard to my next field of labor. I laid all the facts before them in regard to Rochester, and insofar as I was acquainted with them, the leading facts in respect to the other places to which I had been invited at that time. Rochester seemed to be the least inviting of them all.

After talking the matter over and having several seasons of prayer, interspersed with conversation, the brethren gave their opinions one after another in relation to what they thought it wise for me to do. They were unanimous in the opinion that Rochester was too uninviting a place of labor to be put in competition with New York, or Philadelphia, or some other places to which I had been invited. They were firm in the conviction that I should go east from Utica, not west. At the time, this was my own impression and conviction, and I retired from this meeting, as I supposed, settled not to go to Rochester but to New York or Philadelphia. This was before railroads existed, and when we parted that evening I expected to take the canal boat, which was the most convenient way for a family to travel, and start in the morning for New York.

But after I retired to my lodging, the question was presented to my mind from a different viewpoint. Something seemed to question me: "What are the reasons that deter you from going to Rochester?" I could readily enumerate them, but then the question returned: "Ah! but are these good reasons? Certainly you are needed at Rochester all the more because of these difficulties. Do you shun the place because there are so many things that need to be corrected, because there is so much that is wrong? But if all were right, you would not be needed." I soon came to the conclusion that we were all wrong, and that the reasons that had determined us against my going to Rochester were the most cogent reasons for my going! I felt ashamed to shrink from undertaking the work because of its difficulties, and it was strongly impressed upon me that the Lord would be with me and that Rochester was my field. My mind became entirely decided before I retired to rest that Rochester was the place to which the Lord would have me go. I informed my wife of my decision; and accordingly, early in the morning, before the people were generally moving in the city, the packet boat came along, and we embarked and went westward instead of eastward.

The brethren in Utica were greatly surprised when they learned of this change in our destination and awaited the result with a good deal of anxiety.[3]

Question for Thought and Prayer
Do I have a tendency to pray for and expect God to grant me the most pleasing labors in His kingdom?

---

[3]*Autobiography*, 284–86. See the following pages in his *Autobiography* for the amazing revival that occurred in Rochester. John S. Tompkins declared in his article, "Our Kindest City," that because of Finney's revivals: "Twice in half a century, surveys acclaimed Rochester, New York, as the most caring city in America." The "most recent survey was conducted between 1990 and 1992 by Robert V. Levine, chairman of the psychology department at California State University, Fresno." See *Reader's Digest,* July 1994, 53–56.

Chapter 22

Prayer and Conversion

Prevailing or effectual prayer is the prayer that attains the
blessing it seeks.[1]

Soon there were very marked conversions in Rochester. The wife of a
prominent lawyer in that city was one of the first. She was a woman
of high standing, of culture and extensive influence. Her conversion
was very pronounced. The first time I saw her, a friend of hers came
with her to my office and introduced her. The woman making the
introductions was a Christian, who had found that her friend was
under great conviction and persuaded her to come to see me.

The lawyer's wife was an intelligent, worldly-wise woman and very
fond of society. She afterward told me that when I first came to the
city, she greatly regretted it, fearing there would be a revival. She
believed a revival would interfere with the pleasures and amusements
that she had promised herself that winter. Upon conversing with her,
I found that the Spirit of the Lord was indeed dealing with her in an
unsparing manner. She was deeply burdened with great conviction of
sin, and so after a time I pressed her to renounce her sin and the
world and self and everything for Christ. I saw that she was a very
proud woman, and this struck me as the most marked feature of her

---

[1] *Principles of Prayer*, 17.

character. At the conclusion of our conversation, we knelt down to pray, and my mind being full of the subject of the pride of her heart, which seemed obvious, I very soon introduced the text "Unless you change and become like little children, you will never enter the kingdom of heaven" (Matthew 18:3). [Thus I seemed to be led by the Spirit of prayer, almost irresistibly.] I turned this subject over in prayer, and almost immediately heard her at my side repeating the text: "Unless you change and become like little children . . . Unless you change and become like little children." I saw that her mind was taken up with it, and that the Spirit of God was pressing it upon her heart. I therefore continued to pray, holding the subject before her mind and holding her up before God as needing to become as a little child in order to be converted. [I besought the Lord to convert her, to make her as a little child, to put away her pride and her loftiness of spirit and bring her down into the attitude of a child.]

I felt that the Lord was answering us. I felt sure that He was doing the very work I had asked Him to do. Her pride broke down, her confession gushed forth, and before we rose from our knees, she was as a little child. When I stopped praying and opened my eyes to look at her, her face was turned toward heaven and the tears were streaming down; she was in the attitude of praying that she might be made a little child. She rose up, became peaceful, settled into a joyous faith, and left. From that moment she was outspoken in her convictions and zealous for the conversion of her friends. Her conversion, of course, produced quite a stir among that class of people to which she belonged.[2]

Question for Thought and Prayer

Is my pride, or my desire to be looked up to, standing in the way of my prevailing with God in prayer; do I need to be humbled by Him in order to be heard by Him?

---

[2]*Autobiography*, 287–88.

Chapter 23

The Authority of Scripture

Aim to obey perfectly the written law. In other words, have no
fellowship with sin. . . . If you sin at all, let it be your daily grief.
The man who does not aim at this intends to live in sin. Such a
man need not expect God's blessing, for he is not sincere in
desiring to keep all His commandments.[1]

Among other conversions in Rochester, I must not forget to mention that of a prominent citizen who happened to be a bookseller.
This man was an infidel; not an atheist, but a disbeliever in the
divine authority of the Bible. He was a reader and a thinker, a man
with a keen, shrewd mind, strong will, and most decided character. He was, I believe, a man of good outward morals and a gentleman highly respected. He came to my office early one morning
and said to me, "Mr. Finney, there is a great movement here on
the subject of Christianity, but I am a skeptic, and I want you to
prove to me that the Bible is true." The Lord enabled me at once
to discern his state of mind, so far as to decide the course I should
take with him. I said to him, "Do you believe in the existence of

---

[1]*Principles of Prayer*, 76.

God?" "Oh, yes!" he said. "I am not an atheist." "Well, do you believe that you have treated God as you ought? Have you respected His authority? Have you loved Him? Have you done that which you thought would please Him and with the design to please Him? Don't you admit that you ought to love Him, worship Him, and obey Him according to the best light you have?" "Oh, yes!" he said. "I admit all this." "But have you done so?" I asked. "Why no," he answered, "I cannot say that I have." "Well then," I replied, "why should I give you further information and further light if you will not do your duty and obey the light you already have? When you make up your mind to live up to your convictions, to obey God according to the best light you have, and when you make up your mind to repent of your neglect thus far and to please God as well as you know how, I will try to show you that the Bible is from God. Until then it is of no use for me to do so." I did not sit down, and I had not asked him to sit down. He replied, "That is fair," and left.

I heard no more of him until the next morning. Soon after I arose, he came to my door again; and as soon as he entered, he clapped his hands and said, "Mr. Finney, God has wrought a miracle! I went down to the store," he continued, "after I left your place, thinking of what you had said; and I made up my mind that I would repent of what I knew was wrong in my relationship to God, and that hereafter I would live according to the best light I had. And when I made up my mind to do this," he said, "my feelings so overcame me that I fell, and I do not know what would have happened if the storekeeper would not have been there to help me up." From this time forward, this man has been, as all who know him are aware, a praying, earnest Christian. For many years he has been one of the trustees of Oberlin College, has stood by us through all our trials, and has aided us with his means and his influence.[2]

Question for Thought and Prayer
Have I sold out all to the Lord Jesus Christ, resolving to be obedient in all things according to His Word?

---

[2]*Autobiography*, 298–99.

Chapter 24

Praying in the Holy Spirit

Many Christians are so ignorant of the Spirit's influences and have thought so little about having His assistance in prayer that when they have such influences they do not know it and so do not yield to them. They sense nothing unusual in these cases— only the stirring of their minds or the knowledge that their thoughts are intensely employed on a certain subject.[1]

In the morning, after sleeping quietly at a friend's in Auburn, I had arisen and was preparing to take the stage that was to arrive early in the day, when a gentleman came in with the request for me to remain—a request in writing signed by a large number of influential men who had opposed my efforts at revival in 1826 in their city. These men had set themselves against the revival then and had broken from their church. The request in writing was an earnest appeal to me to stop and labor for their salvation, and it was signed by a long list of unconverted men. I was utterly amazed. In this paper they alluded to the opposition they had formerly made to my labors, and begged me to overlook it and stop and preach the gospel to them.

I went to my room and spread the matter before God, and soon made up my mind what to do. I told the pastor and his elders that I

---

[1] *Principles of Prayer*, 70–71.

was nearly exhausted, but that upon certain conditions I would remain. I would preach twice on Sunday and two evenings during the week, but I asked that they would take all the other responsibilities upon themselves. They must not expect me to attend any meetings other than those at which I preached; they must counsel those that came forward; and they must conduct the prayer meetings and any other meetings. I knew that they understood how to deal with sinners, and could well trust them to perform that part of the work.

The decision took immediate effect. On the first or second Sunday evening that I preached, I saw that the Word was taking such powerful hold that at the close I called for those whose minds were made up to come forward, publicly renounce their sins, and give themselves to Christ.[2] Much to my own surprise, and very much to the surprise of the pastor and many members of the church, the first man I observed coming forward and leading the way was the man who had led, and exerted more influence than any other man, in the opposition to the former revival. He came forward promptly, followed by a large number of the persons who had signed that paper; and that evening there was such a demonstration made as to produce a general interest throughout the place.

I have spoken of Mr. Clary as the praying man who was at Rochester.[3] He had a brother, a physician, living in Auburn. I think it was the second Sunday I was at Auburn this time that I noticed in the congregation the solemn face of Mr. Clary. He looked as if he was weighed down with an agony of prayer. Being well acquainted with him, and knowing the great gift of God that was upon him, the spirit of prayer, I was very glad to see him there. He sat in the pew with his brother, the doctor, who was "religious" but who knew nothing by experience of his brother Abel's great power with God.

---

[2]For an excellent description by Charles Finney of the reasons for asking sinners to come forward, see his *Principles of Liberty*, 17.
[3]*Autobiography*, 296–97.

After worship we went to the doctor's house for some refreshments. We gathered around the table, and Dr. Clary turned to his brother and said, "Brother Abel, will you ask a blessing?" Brother Abel bowed his head and began audibly to ask a blessing. He had uttered but a sentence or two when he broke down, moved quickly back from the table, and fled to his room. The doctor supposed he had been taken suddenly ill, and stood up to follow him. In a few moments he came down and said, "Mr. Finney, brother Abel wants to see you." I asked, "What's wrong?" He replied, "I do not know, but he says you know. He appears to be in great distress, but I think it is conviction." I understood it in a moment and went to his room. He lay groaning upon the bed, the Spirit making intercession for him and in him with groanings that could not be uttered. I had barely entered the room when he said to me, "Pray, brother Finney." I knelt down and helped him in prayer by directing his prayers for the conversion of sinners. I continued to pray until his distress passed, and then I returned to the others at the table.

I understood that this was the voice of God. I saw the spirit of prayer was upon him and I felt His influence upon myself, and I took it for granted that the work would move on more powerfully. And it did. I believe, but am not completely sure, that every one of those men who signed that paper, a long list of names, was converted during that revival.[4]

Questions for Thought and Prayer

Are you willing to labor so in prayer for the conversion of souls, even for those whom you do not know, that you would be in great agony of spirit? Or do you prefer to pray that way only for yourself?

---

[4]*Autobiography*, 303–06.

Chapter 25

Revival Lectures and Prayer

He [the Christian] has natural power to pray, and so far as the
will of God is revealed, is able to do it; but he never does unless
the Spirit of God influences him. . . . He [the Holy Spirit] helps
Christians to pray "in accordance with God's will" (Romans
8:27), or for the things that God desires them to pray for.[1]

In January 1834, I was obliged to leave New York on account of my
health and take a sea voyage. I went up the Mediterranean in a small
brig in the midst of winter. We had a very stormy passage. My stateroom was small, and I was on the whole very uncomfortable; and the
voyage did not do much to improve my health. I spent some weeks at
Malta and also in Sicily. I was gone about six months.

On my homeward passage my mind became exceedingly exercised
on the question of revivals. I feared that they would decline throughout the country and that the opposition that had been made to them
had grieved the Holy Spirit. My own health, it appeared to me, had
nearly broken down, and I knew of no other evangelist that would
take the field and aid pastors in revival work. This view of the subject

---

[1]*Principles of Prayer*, 61–62.

distressed me so much that one day I found myself unable to rest. My soul was in utter agony. I spent almost the entire day in prayer [there on my knees] in my stateroom, or walking the deck in [such pain as to wring my hands and almost gnaw my tongue, as it were, for pain and agony] in view of the state of things. In fact, I felt crushed with the burden that was on my soul. There was no one on board to whom I could open my mind or say a word.

It was the spirit of prayer that was upon me, which I had often experienced before, but perhaps never to such a degree or for so long a time. I begged the Lord to go on with His work and to provide those instruments necessary to do so. It was a long summer day in the early part of July, and after the whole day in unspeakable wrestling and agony of soul, at night the subject was clarified to my mind. The Spirit led me to believe that all would come out right, and that God still had work for me to do; that I might be at rest, that the Lord would go forward with His work and give me strength to take any part in it that He desired. But I had no idea what the course of His providence would be.

(*Editor's Note:* Finney continues in his account to explain why he was commissioned to preach a series of lectures on revival for his New York congregation and for publication in the *New York Evangelist*. These lectures contain most of his principles of prayer. He then proceeds with his account of God's blessing on these lectures. The full record of the circumstances can be found in *Principles of Prayer*, 117–21.)

These lectures were later published in a book called *Finney's Lectures on Revival*. Twelve thousand copies were sold, as fast as they could be printed. And here, for the glory of Christ, I can say that they have been reprinted in England and France. They were translated into Welsh; and on the continent were translated into French and, I believe, into German; they were very extensively circulated throughout Europe and the colonies of Great Britain. They were, I presume, to be found wherever the English language is spoken. After they had been printed in Welsh, the Congregational ministers of the principality of Wales, at one of their public meetings, appointed a committee to inform me of the great revival that had resulted from the translation of those lectures into the Welsh language. This they did by letter. One publisher in London informed me that his father had published eighty thousand volumes of them. [I do not know into how many languages they have been translated. But I mention this particularly as being an answer to prayer.] These revival lectures, meager as was the report of them, and weak as they were in themselves, have been instrumental, as I have learned, in promoting revivals in England, Scotland, Wales, on the continent in various places, in Canada, east and west, in Nova Scotia, and in some of the islands of the sea.

In England and Scotland I have often been encouraged by meeting with ministers and laymen in great numbers who had been converted directly or indirectly through the instrumentality of those lectures. I recall that the last time I was abroad, one evening three very prominent ministers of the gospel introduced themselves to me after the sermon and said that when they were in college they read my revival lectures, which had resulted in their becoming ministers. I found persons in England, in many different denominations, who had not only read those revival lectures but had also been greatly blessed in reading them. When they were first published in the *New York Evangelist*, the reading of them resulted in revivals of religion in many places throughout the country.

But this was not of man's wisdom. The reader will remember that long day of agony and prayer at sea that God would do something to forward the work of revivals, and enable me, if He desired to do it, to take such a course as to help the work move forward. I felt certain then that my prayers would be answered; and I have regarded all that

I have since been able to accomplish, [and all the results of preaching and publishing those lectures, as well as all else that I have been in any wise instrumental in accomplishing for the kingdom of God, is in a very important sense an answer to the prayers of that day. It has always been my experience that when I have a day or season of great travail of soul for any object, if I pursue the subject, and continue my pleadings until I prevail and my soul is at rest, that in answer to such prayers God not only gives me what I ask, but exceedingly above all that I at the time had in my mind. God has been answering the prayers of that day on shipboard for more than thirty years.[2]

Nobody but myself can appreciate the wonderful manner in which those agonizing throes of my soul on that occasion have met with the divine response. Indeed, it was God, the Holy Spirit, asking intercession in me. The prayer was not properly mine, but the prayer of the Holy Spirit. It was no righteousness or worthiness of my own at all.][3] The spirit of prayer came upon me as a sovereign grace, bestowed upon me without the least merit and despite all of my sinfulness. He pressed my soul in prayer until I was enabled to prevail, and through the infinite riches of grace in Christ Jesus, I have been many years witnessing the wonderful results of that day of wrestling with God. In answer to that day's agony, He has continued to give me the spirit of prayer.[4]

---

[2]I believe that God is even now answering the prayer that Finney offered so long ago. There is still much interest in and study of his principles of prayer and revival. Jonathan Goforth says of Finney's influence upon him and the revivals in China: "Selections from *Finney's Autobiography* and *Revival Lectures* were sent to me by a friend in India (the fall of 1905). It was the final something which set me on fire. . . . 'If Finney is right,' I vowed, 'then I'm going to find out what those laws are and obey them, no matter what it costs' " (Jonathan Goforth, *By My Spirit* [Minneapolis: Bethany House, 1964], 19–20).

[3]Of course, Finney would not have denied that his own agency was important in responding to the leading of the Spirit of God. These words express his humility and praise for the work of God.

[4]*Autobiography*, 325, 328–31.

Question for Thought and Prayer

If God desires to do such great things for us and for His kingdom on earth in answer to prayer, why are my efforts and time spent on my knees so weak?

Chapter 26

Perfection

The soul of a Christian, when it is thus burdened, must have relief. God rolls this weight upon the soul of a Christian for the purpose of bringing him nearer to himself.[1]

The *Lectures on Revivals of Religion* were preached while I was still pastor of the Presbyterian Church in Chatham Street Chapel. The two following winters I gave lectures to Christians in the Broadway Tabernacle, which were also reported by Mr. Leavitt and published in the *New York Evangelist.* These also have been printed in a volume in this country and in Europe.[2] Those sermons to Christians were very much the result of a searching that was going on in my own mind. I mean that the Spirit of God was showing me many things in regard to the question of sanctification that led me to preach these sermons to Christians.

Many Christians regarded those lectures as an exhibition of the law rather than the gospel. But I did not and do not so regard them. For

---

[1] *Principles of Prayer*, 36.
[2] The sermons that Finney is referring to are published in his *Lectures to Professing Christians* (London: Milner and Company, 1837). Two of these sermons with the title "Christian Perfection" on the text Matthew 5:48 are included in Charles G. Finney, *Principles of Holiness* (Minneapolis: Bethany House Publishers, 1984) 17–53 (currently out of print).

me, the law and the gospel have but one rule of life, and every violation of the spirit of the law is also a violation of the spirit of the gospel. But I have long been satisfied that the higher forms of Christian experience are attained only as a result of a serious searching application of God's law to the human conscience and heart. The result of my labors up to that time had shown me more clearly than I had known before the great weakness of Christians and that the older members of the church, in general, were making very little progress in grace. I found that they would fall back from a revival state even sooner than the young converts. It had been so in the revival in which I was converted. I saw clearly that this was due to their early teaching; that is, to the views that they had been led to entertain when they were young converts.

I was also led into a state of great dissatisfaction with my own lack of stability in faith and love. To tell the truth, I must say to the praise of God's grace that He did not allow me to backslide to the extent to which many Christians did. But I often felt weak in the presence of temptation and needed frequently to hold days of fasting and prayer and to spend much time in renewing my own life in order to retain that communion with God and that hold upon the divine strength that would enable me to labor efficiently for the promotion of revival.

In looking at the state of the Christian church as it had been revealed to me in my revival labors, I was led earnestly to inquire whether there was not something higher and more enduring than the Christian church was aware of; whether there were not promises and means provided in the gospel for the establishment of Christians in an altogether higher form of Christian life. I had known somewhat of the view of sanctification entertained by our Methodist brethren. But as their idea of sanctification seemed to me to relate almost entirely to states of the emotions, I could not receive their teaching. However, I gave myself earnestly to searching the Scriptures and to reading whatever came into my hand on the subject until my mind was satisfied that a higher and more stable form of Christian life was attainable and was the privilege of all Christians.

This led me to preach in the Broadway Tabernacle two sermons on Christian perfection.[3] In those sermons I defined what Christian perfection is and endeavored to show that it is attainable in this life and how it is attainable. [These sermons were published in the *New York Evangelist*. So far as I know they did not startle the Christian church as anything heretical, for until some time after I came to Oberlin, I never heard a question of the truth of those sermons raised in any quarter.] But about this time the question of Christian perfection in the antinomian sense (belief that the Christian is free of all forms of the law) of the term was heatedly discussed at New Haven, Albany, and somewhat in New York City. I examined these views as published in the periodical entitled *The Perfectionist*. But I could not accept them. Yet I was satisfied that the doctrine of sanctification in this life, and entire sanctification in the sense that it was the privilege of Christians to live without known sin, was a doctrine taught in the Bible, and that abundant means were provided for the securing of that attainment.

The last winter I spent in New York, the Lord was pleased to visit my soul with a great refreshing. After a period of heart searching, He brought me, as He has often done, into a new awareness of himself and gave me much of that divine sweetness in my soul of which Jonathan Edwards speaks as attained in his own experience. That winter I had a time of thorough repentance in my own life, so much so that sometimes for a considerable period I could not refrain from loud weeping in view of my own sins and of the love of God in Christ. Such seasons were frequent that winter, and resulted in the great renewal of my spiritual strength and enlargement of my views in

---

[3]When Finney went to Oberlin, he preached another series on perfection, and these are found in *The Promise of the Spirit*, edited by Timothy L. Smith, and published by Bethany House (currently out of print).

regard to the privileges of Christians and the abundance of the grace of God.[4]

Question for Thought and Prayer

Have you ever thoroughly examined your life according to the law of God, confessed your sins, and rejoiced that Jesus Christ has given you victory over all known sin?

---

[4]*Autobiography*, 339–41.

Chapter 27

Total Commitment

Test the spirits by the Bible. . . . If you compare them faithfully
with the Bible, you never need be led astray. You can always
know whether your feelings are produced by the Spirit's
influence by comparing your desires with the spirit and tone of
religion as described in the Bible. . . . The Spirit of God
influences the mind . . . He enlightens the intelligence and leads
the Christian who is under His influence to be eminently
reasonable and rational in all his outlook and actions.[1]

During the winter of 1843, the Lord gave my soul a very thorough
spiritual overhauling and a fresh baptism of His Spirit. I boarded at
the Marlborough Hotel in Boston, and my study and bedroom were
in one corner of the chapel building. My mind was greatly drawn out
in prayer for a long time, as indeed it always has been when I have
labored in Boston. I have been favored there with a great deal of the
spirit of prayer. But this winter in particular my mind was exceedingly
exercised on the question of personal holiness; in respect to the state
of the church, their lack of power with God; the weakness of the
orthodox churches in Boston, the weakness of their faith, and their
lack of power in the midst of such a community. The fact that they

[1] *Principles of Prayer*, 73–74.

were making little or no progress in overcoming the errors of that city greatly affected my mind.

I gave myself to a great deal of prayer. After my evening services, I would retire as early as I could, but rose at four o'clock in the morning because I could sleep no longer and immediately went to the study and prayed. So deeply was I exercised, and so absorbed in prayer, that I frequently continued from the time I arose at four o'clock until the gong called to breakfast at eight o'clock. My days were spent, so far as I could get time, in searching the Scriptures [for I had a great deal of company coming constantly to see me]. I read nothing else all that winter but my Bible; and a great deal of it seemed new to me. Again the Lord took me, as it were, from Genesis to Revelation. He led me to see the connection of things, the promises, the warnings, the prophecies and their fulfillment; and indeed, the whole Scripture seemed to be ablaze with light, and not only light, but it seemed as if God's Word was permeated with the very life of God.

After praying in this way for weeks and months, one morning while I was engaged in prayer, the thought occurred to me, *What if after all this divine teaching, my will is not convinced, and the teaching takes effect only in my emotions? Can it be that my emotions are affected by these revelations from the Bible and that my heart is not really subdued by them?* At this point several passages of Scripture occurred to me, such as "Do and do, do and do, rule on rule, rule on rule; a little here, a little there—so that they will go and fall backward, be injured and snared and captured" (Isaiah 28:13). The thought that I might be deceiving myself [by the states of my feelings], when it first occurred to me, stung me almost like an adder. It created a pain that I cannot describe. The passages of Scripture that occurred to me in that direction for a few moments greatly increased my distress. But immediately I was enabled to fall back upon the perfect will of God. I said to the Lord that if He saw it was wise and best, and that His honor demanded that I should be left to be deluded and go down to hell, I accepted His will, and I said to Him, "Do with me as seems good to thee."

Just before this happened, I struggled to consecrate myself to God in a higher sense than I had ever before seen to be my duty or conceived as possible. I had often before laid all my family upon the altar of God and left them to be disposed of at His discretion. But at this time that I speak of, I had a great struggle about giving up my wife to the will of God. She was in very frail health, and it was evident that she could not live long. I had never before seen so clearly what was implied in laying her and all that I possessed upon the altar of God. For hours I struggled upon my knees to give her up totally to the will of God. But I found myself unable to do it. I was so shocked and surprised at this that I perspired profusely with agony. I struggled and prayed until I was exhausted, and found myself entirely unable to give her up completely to God's will in such a way as to make no objection to His disposing of her just as He pleased.

This troubled me considerably. I wrote to my wife, telling her what a struggle I had and the concern that I felt at not being willing to commit her without reserve to the perfect will of God. This was only a short time before I had the temptation of which I spoke when those passages of Scripture came up distressingly to my mind and when the bitterness almost of death seemed for a few moments to possess me at the thought that my faith might be of emotions only and that God's teaching might have taken effect only in my feelings. But as I said, I was enabled, after struggling for a few moments with this discouragement and bitterness, which I have since attributed to a fiery dart of Satan, to fall back in a deeper sense than I had ever done before upon the infinitely blessed and perfect will of God. I then told the Lord that I had such confidence in Him that I felt perfectly willing to give myself, my wife, and my family, all to be disposed of [without any qualification] according to His own [views and will. That if He thought it best and wise to send me to hell, to do so, and I would consent to it. As to my wife, I felt entirely willing to lay her body and soul upon the altar without the least misgiving in my mind in delivering her up to the perfect will of God.]

I then had a deeper view than ever before of what was implied in consecration to God. I spent a long time on my knees considering the matter again and giving up everything to the will of God: the interests of the church, the progress of Christianity, the conversion of the world, and the salvation or damnation of my own soul, as the will of God might decide. Indeed, I remember that I went so far as to say to the Lord, with all my heart, that He might do anything with me or mine to which His blessed will could consent. I had such perfect confidence in His goodness and love as to believe that He could consent to do nothing to which I could object. I felt a kind of holy boldness in telling Him to do with me just as seemed to Him good; that He could not do anything that was not perfectly wise and good; therefore, I had the best of grounds for accepting whatever He could consent to in respect to me and mine. So deep and perfect a resting in His will I had never known before.

What has appeared strange to me is this, that I could not get hold of my former hope; nor could I recollect with any freshness any of the former seasons of communion and divine assurance that I had experienced. I may say that I gave up hope and rested everything upon a new foundation. I mean, I gave up my hope from any past experience, and recall telling the Lord that I did not know whether He intended to save me or not. Nor did I feel concerned to know. I was willing to abide the event. I said that if I found that He kept me, and worked in me by His Spirit, and was preparing me for heaven, working holiness and eternal life in my soul, I would take it for granted that He intended to save me. That if, on the other hand, I found myself empty of divine strength and light and love, I would conclude that He saw it wise and expedient to send me to hell. In either event I would accept His will. My mind settled into a perfect stillness.

This was early in the morning, and through the whole of that day I seemed to be in a state of perfect rest, body and soul. The question frequently arose in my mind during the day, "Do you still adhere to your consecration and abide in the will of God?" I said without hesitation, "Yes, I take nothing back. I have no reason to take anything back. I went no further in oaths and promises than was reasonable." The thought that I might be lost did not distress me. Indeed, think as I might, during that whole day I could not find in my mind the least fear, the least disturbing emotion. Nothing troubled me. I was neither elated nor depressed. I was neither joyful nor sorrowful. My confidence in God was perfect. My acceptance of His will was perfect, and my mind was as calm as heaven.

Then at evening the question arose in my mind, *What if God should send me to hell, what then? Why, I would not object to it. But can He send a person to hell*, was the next inquiry, *who accepts His will in the sense in which you do?* This inquiry was no sooner raised in my mind than settled. I said, "No, it is impossible. Hell could be no hell to me if I accepted God's perfect will." This sprung a vein of joy within me that kept developing more and more for weeks and months, and indeed I may say, for years. For years I was too full of joy to feel much anxiety on any subject. My prayer that had been so fervent and protracted during so long a period, seemed all to run out into "Thy will be done." It seemed as if my desires were all met. What I had been praying for, for myself, I had received in a way that I least expected. Holiness to the Lord seemed to be inscribed in all my thoughts and activities. I had such strong faith that God would accomplish all His perfect will that I could not worry about anything. The great anxieties about which my mind had been exercised during my seasons of agonizing prayer seemed to be set aside; so that for a long time, when I went to God to commune with Him—as I did very frequently—I would fall on my knees and find it impossible to ask for anything with any earnestness, except that His will might be done on earth as it is done in heaven. My prayers were swallowed up in that. I often found myself smiling, as it were, in the face of God, and saying that I did not want anything. I was very sure that He would accomplish all His wise and good pleasure, and with that my soul was entirely satisfied.

Here I lost that great struggle in which I had been engaged for so long and began to preach to the congregation in accordance with this new and enlarged experience. There was a considerable number in the church that attended my preaching who understood me. They saw from my preaching what had been and what was now passing in my mind. I presume the people were more aware than I was of the great change in my manner of preaching. Of course, my mind was too full of the subject to preach anything except a full and present salvation in the Lord Jesus Christ.

At this time it seemed as if my soul was wedded to Christ in a sense in which I had never had any thought or conception before. The language of the Song of Solomon was as natural to me as my breath. I thought I could understand well the state of mind he was in when he wrote that song; and concluded then, as I have thought ever since, that the song was written after he had been reclaimed from his great backsliding. I not only had all the freshness of my first love but also a greater appreciation of it. Indeed, the Lord lifted me so much above anything that I had experienced before, and taught me so much of the meaning of the Bible, of Christ's power, and willingness to relate to us, that I often found myself saying to Him, "I had not known or conceived that any such thing was true." I then realized what is meant by the word "He is able to do exceeding abundantly above all that we ask or think." He did at that time teach me infinitely above all that I had ever asked or thought. I had before no concept of the length and breadth, the height and depth, and the efficiency of His grace.

It seemed to me then that the passage "My grace is sufficient for you" (2 Corinthians 12:9) meant so much more; I had never understood it before. I found myself exclaiming, "Wonderful! Wonderful!

Wonderful!" as these revelations were made to me. I could understand what was meant by the prophet when he said, "And he will be called Wonderful Counselor, Mighty God, Everlasting Father, Prince of Peace" (Isaiah 9:6). I spent nearly all the remaining part of the winter, until I was obliged to return home, in instructing the people in regard to the fullness there is in Christ. But I found that I preached over the heads of the majority of the people. They did not understand me. Thankfully, however, there was indeed a godly number that did, and they were wonderfully blessed in their souls and made more progress in the divine life, I have reason to believe, than in all their lives before.

As the great excitement of that season subsided and I became more calm, I saw more clearly the different steps of my Christian experience and came to recognize the connection of things as all wrought by God from beginning to end. But since then I have never had these great struggles and long protracted seasons of agonizing prayer [before I could get hold of full rest in God] that I had often experienced. It is quite another thing to prevail with God in my own experience from what it was before. I can come to God with greater calmness because I come with more perfect confidence. He enables me now to rest in Him and let everything sink into His perfect will with much more readiness than ever before the experience of that winter.

I have felt since then a greater freedom, a buoyancy and delight in God and in His Word, a steadiness of faith, a Christian liberty, and overflowing love that I had only occasionally experienced before. I do not mean that such experiences had been rare to me before, for they had been frequent and often repeated, but never abiding as they have been since. My bondage seemed to be at that time entirely broken. And since then I have had the freedom of a child with a loving parent. It seems to me that I can find God within me in such a sense that I can rest upon Him and be quiet, lay my heart in His hand and nestle down in His perfect will and have no worry or anxiety.

I speak of these exercises as habitual since that period, but I cannot affirm that they have been entirely unbroken; for in 1860, during a period of sickness, I had a season of great depression and humiliation. But the Lord brought me out of it into an established peace and rest.[2]

Question for Thought and Prayer

Have I so committed my all to the Lord, and so consecrated myself to Him and His service, that I am willing and able to receive whatever future He intends for me from His hand?

[2]*Autobiography*, 374–81.

Chapter 28

Quenching the Holy Spirit

If you have much of the Spirit of God, you must make up your
mind to have much opposition, both in the church and in the
world. . . . Often the elders, and even the minister, will oppose
you if you are filled with the Spirit of God. You must expect
very frequent and agonizing conflicts with Satan. Satan has very
little trouble with those Christians who are not spiritual but
lukewarm, slothful, and worldly-minded. And these have no
concept of what spiritual conflict is.[1]

[After spending a few weeks in Detroit in 1846, in compliance with
the earnest request of the church at Pontiac, I went there for a season.
At Pontiac I found a very unusual and trying state of things. The place
had first been settled by a class of infidels who were scoffers of religion. But there were several pious women in the neighborhood, and
after a great struggle they finally prevailed to have religious meetings
established and had built a church and found a minister. There was
then living in Pontiac the man who had been the pastor of the church
immediately preceding the brother who was there at the time I went.
The young man who was pastor when I arrived was from New
England. I do not recall his name. With the former pastor, the church

---

[1] *Principles of Prayer*, 90.

had great difficulty. They had become very divided in respect to him and finally dismissed him. But the circumstances had been such as to leave a very bad feeling between him and the church and also between him and another elder minister, who lived close to the village and who had labored a good deal as a missionary in that new area in establishing churches. This former missionary had taken a very active part in the controversy between the old pastor and the church, so that between him and the old pastor there was no ministerial or even Christian sympathy. Indeed, I found the state of things about as unpromising and difficult to manage as I had ever seen anywhere. However, I began to preach, and it was soon evident that the Spirit of God was greatly searching the church. I began there, as I usually did, to have the hindrances to revival removed, mutual confession, and restitution attended to, and in short to reconvert the church and prepare the way for a general revival among the openly impenitent. The state of morals at that time in Pontiac was low.

The people were enterprising, and the place was thrifty from a business standpoint; but true Christianity was at the lowest ebb. I saw that nothing effectual could be done until the old roots of bitterness were extracted, their divisions healed, and their animosities put away.

I therefore addressed my preaching to the church and to the professing Christians, and preached as boldly to them as I could. That was the home of their Lieutenant Governor Richardson. His wife was a religious woman, but had been drawn considerably into the great controversy between their old pastor and the church. After preaching for a week or two, I thought the way was sufficiently prepared, and it was agreed to set apart a day for fasting, humbling, and prayer. When the day arrived, I preached to them from this text: "O Hope of Israel, its Savior ... why are you like a stranger in the land, like a traveler who stays only a night?" (Jeremiah 14:8). I was greatly concerned with the application of this text to the present condition of the people. In the afternoon we had a general prayer meeting of the church. Soon after the meeting began, it was evident to me that the Holy Spirit was present in a powerful way. I was the guest of a Mr. Davis, who had taken a very prominent part in the controversy with their former pastor. He was a man of strong opinions and had been most hostile in his feelings toward the pastor, placing full blame on him. The old pastor was a near neighbor to him. As we came home from the morning service, I saw that Mr. Davis was very deeply convicted. He said to me, "Don't you think it would be best for me to go and make confession to that minister? He was wrong, but I have had a very bad attitude toward him." I inquired, "Can you go and confess to him without reproaching him, leaving him to confess his own sins?" He said he could, and immediately he left the house, went over, and as I understood, made a humble confession without accusing him at all. He told him that he had entertained very unchristian feelings toward him and asked his forgiveness.

As I said, soon after we assembled in the afternoon it was evident that there was a spirit of great conviction on the congregation. Their former pastor was present, as I believe he was every time we held a meeting. Soon after we had assembled, I observed Mrs. Richardson rise from her seat and pass around the church to the opposite side where her old pastor sat and openly confessed to him that she had entertained very unchristian feelings toward him. This had a remarkable effect on those present. I observed that the pastor's face turned deadly pale. As soon as Mrs. Richardson turned away, there was quite a general movement from different parts of the house of persons going to his seat to confess to him. I saw how the work was going on, and felt confident that there would be a general humbling of those present.

From the manifest impression that it was making upon their old pastor, I expected any moment to see him go to his knees and make confession. The pressure at this time upon the congregation was tremendous. I kept entirely still, and so also did their new pastor, the young man. But just at this moment, the old missionary, whose name I think was Ruggles, arose and objected to what was going on. He opposed it, he said, because their old pastor, calling him by name, would triumph and say that the congregation had justified him and condemned themselves. I did not believe then, nor do I now, that there was the least danger of that. I think if Father Ruggles, as they called him, had kept still, it would not have been ten minutes before the pastor would have made as full a confession as they could have desired. However, Father Ruggles was too strongly committed against the old pastor to allow anything being done that could by any possibility be construed into a justification of the pastor's course and a condemnation of the course that his church had pursued toward him. The moment Father Ruggles took this position, a distinct reaction came over the meeting. All confession ceased; all tears were wiped away; and I never in any meeting in my life saw so manifest a quenching of the Holy Spirit's influence as was obvious there.

The reaction was instantaneous and decisive. Up to that moment all their animosities were melted away, but this mistaken course of Father Ruggles brought the rising spirit of confession to a halt, totally reversed its course, and tore the old wounds open once again. After looking at the desolation for a few days, I returned to Detroit, where I was taken sick, and for a number of days confined to my bed. The season had arrived for opening our spring term at Oberlin, and as soon as I was able to travel I returned home, and as usual commenced my labors here; and we had a very interesting revival through the summer.][2]

Question for Thought and Prayer

Through unconfessed sin and animosity, am I stifling revival in my church and hindering God from answering my prayers?

---

[2]From the unpublished manuscript of the *Autobiography*, 385–86.

Chapter 29

Finney's Vision Near Death

To be sure, He [God] often does more than answer prayer. He grants them not only what they ask but also connects other blessings with it.[1]

[That summer (1847) I published the second volume of my *Systematic Theology*. I wrote it out and published it, and attended to my college and pastoral duties. Most of the second volume I wrote at the rate of a lecture a day and sent it to the printers, so that I would correct the proof of one lecture and write another and send it to the press the same day. But this, with all my pastoral duties, and my intense labors in my classes, so used up my strength that on commencement evening I was taken with typhus fever. For two months I was very sick and came very near death. Meanwhile, my precious wife was failing with tuberculosis. About the middle of December she passed away. When she died, my strength had not returned, and I stayed at home that winter and did not perform much ministerial labor here or elsewhere. I resumed my labors as pastor and professor too soon to favor a rapid return to strength.

---

[1] *Principles of Prayer*, 54.

For this reason, I remained at home through the winter of 1847–48, not feeling able to perform the labors of an evangelist abroad.]

The following are notations by Finney's wife during his illness in 1847:

Wednesday, 25th August—Addressed his graduating class. Came home totally exhausted. But went out in the evening and attended a meeting of the trustees. When he came home, sat down and talked a little while with Mrs. Blake. Complained of great pain in his head and uncommon exhaustion. Rested very little during the night.

26th—Thought he would get up but found himself unable to dress, and went to bed again. Great restlessness through the day. Took nothing into his mouth, not even a drop of water.

27th—A restless night, severe pains in the head and back, and continued through the day. Said, "Oh, how sweet it would be to be undisturbed in the grave, no pain, none of this restlessness. But I can't die, I shall never die." Talked with me about the making of his will. Said that he had sometimes thought that it looked so much as though he felt the property that he held in his name was his own. But when he became sick that the law would recognize it as his. He felt that he might as well dispose of it as for the law to do it, and accordingly he got Mr. Parish of Sandusky to write it in the afternoon.

28th—Seemed more comfortable in the morning, sat up for a few moments. Still his restlessness continues. Said, "I do not want to live, I am ready to go," and with a sweet smile added, "You, my dear, will soon go too."

29th, Sabbath—His birthday. Passed a horrible night. His mind so active that he could not rest. His sleep a kind of dreamy consciousness, partly of life and partly of death. Said to the doctor, "I am a poor patient for you, for I am entirely exhausted, my strength is all gone. It seems all but impossible to get up again."

Said he had thought out a great many books during the night.

30th—Evidently worse, had an awfully distressing night, as he expressed it all night, "Sweet to be in the hands of the Lord." Said, "I don't know whether Dr. Jenning(?) is right or not; in any case, I have no confidence in any other theory. It is the best light I have." Gave directions about a great many things, what I had better do under such and such circumstances. Talked about appointing a guardian for the boys, especially little Norton. Said that every system of moral philosophy was fundamentally false.

31st—His system more quiet, slept some, P.M. When he awoke, said, "What profound rest. No words can describe the sweet peace. Thank the Lord my mind is calm, nothing is suffered to disturb its deep repose. I shall soon see William, and if we get to discussing the great subjects, we should get light fast."

With regard to a certain subject, said he had said unkind and unwise things to a few individuals. Still he looked at the facts and the developments just as he did at the time. But the Lord enabled him last winter to leave it all to the judgment and let it rest there. Said, "My dear, I have often grieved you, but I know that I have your forgiveness, and I am not troubled. Jesus saves me from all anxiety."

When I said, "Charles is no better, and Norton was most sick, and that Rebecca was unable to sit up, threatened with a fever," he said, "What a blessed thing for us all to die together. It seems to me as if I am going to die. I am making all my arrangements for those I am going to leave, though I have not thought much about the place where I am going. Still I had this morning a view of how heaven was lighted. It was imagination, I presume. But such splendid columns and palisades, their tops enveloped in such glorious light, and yet there was no sun. A little glimpse of heaven, imagination, I suppose. I don't know yet, perhaps not. Sweet Jesus, sweet Jesus, I have wanted to write more books, but how sweet this passage, 'Seal up what the seven thunders have said and do not write it down' (Revelation 10:4)."[2]

Question for Thought and Prayer

Is my relationship with God through faith in Jesus Christ such that I could approach death, calling, "Sweet Jesus, sweet Jesus"?

---

[2]The first part of this sketch should be inserted prior to page 386 in the *Autobiography*. The account by Finney's wife appears in the back pages of one of Finney's old pastoral theology notebooks, believed to be of his lectures in the 1840s, catalogued 091.25, F 497 C. It is written in pencil, and is hard to read in places.

Chapter 30

The Consequences of Apostasy

If you die without the Spirit, you will fall into hell. There can be
no doubt about this. Without the Spirit you will never be
prepared for heaven.[1]

[A circumstance occurred during this revival relating to the celebrated
Theodore Parker, who held services in a large hall in Boston, and
whose views of theology and religion are so well understood that I
need not enter into particulars in regard to them. During this winter,
a good many Christian people became stirred up in their minds about
the evil influence that he was exerting in Boston, and there was much
prayer offered for him. I called twice to see him, hoping to have an
opportunity to converse with him, but in both instances he declined
to see me, declaring it was due to the state of his health.

But the spirit of prayer for him seemed to increase and took on
this tone: that the Lord would convert him if He wisely could, but that
if He could not do this, that at least his evil influence might in some
way be set aside. God's people labored so much upon this point that
a number of Christian gentlemen met by appointment in a certain

---

[1]*Principles of Prayer*, 99.

place to lay this matter before God. I state the facts as they were told me by one of the gentlemen present. He said that after the meeting was opened, they called on one of their number to lead in prayer, and he led out in prayer in such a remarkable manner—laid the whole subject so fully before God—and in such a spirit as to lead them all with one heart and one soul to unite in laying the whole case before God. He said the man who led in prayer seemed almost to be inspired, to say just the right things and in the right way and spirit as he led them.

They all felt as if their prayer would be answered; and so deep was this impression, that although they had come together for a prayer, after the first prayer was offered no one had a word to say. He said that the feeling was unanimous that they had prayed enough, that the answer to their prayer was certain, and that no more prayer was necessary; and none of them felt inclined to offer any further petition to God about it. In some way this prayer meeting came to the knowledge of Dr. Parker, and he said, and I believe wrote, some very strong things against it. However, he soon became very ill, was unable to preach, went to Europe for his health, and there died. Thus ended the evil influence of his preaching forever, except as the remembrance of it may influence future generations.][2]

Question for Thought and Prayer

When I pray, am I fully aware of the awesome power of prayer in those who are fully consecrated Christian people?

---

[2]To be inserted following page 444 in the *Autobiography*. Theodore Parker was a Unitarian preacher, 1810–1860. It is of this passage in the handwritten manuscript, which was edited by Fairchild for publication, that Fairchild wrote, "Dear Bro. S. Read this with Bro. W. and tell me whether it should go in."

Appendix A

Professor Wright's Observations

The following observations regarding Finney's public prayer life, including some examples of his prayers, are made by G. Frederick Wright, Professor of Oberlin Theological Seminary, Oberlin, Ohio, and are taken from his biography of Finney: *Charles Grandison Finney* (Boston and New York: Houghton and Mifflin and Company, 1891), 274–79. Wright's biography gives an excellent analysis of both Finney's life and theology.

Finney's prayers were always a most interesting and inspiring part of the public services at Oberlin. Apparently he prayed in public as he did in private, forgetful that any were present beside himself and his Creator. His petitions for the afflicted and needy of the parish were particularly touching and tender. He seemed to have every individual always before his mind. The students can never forget how when the autumn term drew to a close and they were about to face the trials of teaching in the winter schools throughout the region, his prayers for them would increase in fervency as he sought the Lord to keep the "dear children from misfortune and evil, and to gird them with strength for their trying work."[1] His petitions were entirely free from

---

[1] G. F. Wright's own autobiography relates very touchingly the difficulties he encountered as a winter teacher from Oberlin. These winter students had a great influence and spread their concern for the abolition of slavery throughout the country. See G. Frederick Wright, *Story of My Life and Work* (Oberlin: Bibliotheca Sacra Co.), 1916.

formality, were usually limited to objects of immediate interest, and only on occasion included the country and the world at large. Apparently he relied much upon the direct leading of the Holy Spirit in prayer, and this childlike spirit must be kept in mind if we would properly understand the significance of some of the immediate answers that came. Probably his aversion to uttering many of the ordinary general petitions arose from his doctrine respecting the "prayer of faith." In his lecture on that subject he replies in answer to the question of when we are to offer this prayer: "When you have evidence from promises, or prophecies, or providences, or the leading of the Spirit that God will do the things you pray for. You have no evidence that it is God's will to convert the whole world at once." Some of his remarkable prayers for rain can scarcely be accounted for except by the explanation that he was led by the Spirit.

For example, the summer of 1853 was unusually hot and dry, so that the pastures were scorched and there seemed likely to be a total failure of the crops. Under these circumstances, the great congregation gathered one Sunday in the church at Oberlin as usual, when, though the sky was clear, the burden of Finney's prayer was for rain. In his prayer he deepened the cry of distress that went up from every heart by mentioning in detail the consequences of prolonged drought. In essence, these were his words:

"We do not presume, O Lord, to dictate to thee what is best for us; yet thou dost invite us to come to thee as children to a father and tell thee all our wants. We want rain. Our pastures are dry. The earth is gaping open for rain. The cattle are wandering about and lowing in search of water. Even the little squirrels in the woods are suffering from thirst. Unless thou givest us rain, our cattle will die and our harvests will come to nought. O Lord, send us rain, and send it now! Although to us there is no sign of it, it is an easy thing for thee to do. Send it now, Lord, for Christ's sake! Amen."[2]

[2]Rev. Joseph Adams in *Reminiscences* (no publication data), 55–56.

Says a correspondent, the Rev. O. B. Waters, in describing the remainder of the scene, "I remember, as distinctly as yesterday, the prolongation, the fervency, the urgency, the heartfelt pleadings of those petitions. I remember that at length he closed, took his text, and preached perhaps ten or fifteen minutes, when we began to hear the patter upon the roof. I remember that he preached a few minutes longer; that the rattle and the roar increased; that suddenly he stopped and said, 'I think we had better thank God for the rain.' And when he indicated the hymn "When all thy mercies, O my God! My rising soul surveys," the whole congregation rose up and sang it; the rain continued, so that when at last we were dismissed at the noon hour, multitudes stood around and waited until the full skies could pour out their abounding floods."

At another time he prayed for rain in the following words: "O Lord, the long-looked-for clouds are at last over our heads, and we pray that they may now burst, and deluge the parched earth. Do not let them pass by and discharge their waters upon the lake, as they have done so often of late, for thou knowest, O Lord, that there is already water enough in the lake." The effect of this prayer is not related.

But occasionally his irrepressible humor came to the surface in the prayers with which he habitually closed the hour of classroom work. At one time, when for some reason the class met for a few days in his study, one or two of them yielded to the hypnotic effect of the well-cushioned seats and fell asleep. In his closing prayer, Finney did not forget these unfortunate members, but prayed that they might hereafter be kept awake. When the class came into the room the next day, they found the easy chairs replaced by hard-seated chairs from the kitchen. Finney good-humoredly remarked to them, "You see, young gentlemen, I have found a way to answer my own prayer."

At another time, when he had been dwelling at great length upon technical questions of theology, and when the danger was great of the students' getting merely the form of sound words without their power,

Finney closed the hour with the prayer that the Lord would mellow their hearts and give life and power to the truth; for, if He did not, their whole system of theology "would be so dry that it would be fit only to choke a moral agent."

On another day, when the class in theology had been quite eloquent in expressing their own views, Finney in closing prayed, "O Lord, do not let these young men think that because they have let down a little line into the infinite sea of thy greatness, they have sounded all its depths! Save them from conceit, O Lord!"

When the National Congregational Council was organized at Oberlin, advantage was taken of its presence to dedicate the building for the theological seminary (named from the event Council Hall), though it was then only partially completed. Finney was asked to make the dedicatory prayer. Before beginning his prayer he said, "I have felt somewhat embarrassed with regard to performing this part of the service because the house is not entirely finished. I have several times refused to take part in dedicating a house of worship that was not paid for; but this is neither finished nor paid for, and hence I have had some hesitation about offering it to God in this state. But I remember that I have often offered myself to God, and I am far from being finished yet, and why should I not offer this house just as it is? I will do so, relying upon the determination of those having the charge to finish it as soon as possible."[3]

In general, Finney respected the rule for which he voted in the New Lebanon Convention that it was improper to pray by name for persons in public without their permission. But I remember hearing him pray for a particular professor in a somewhat extraordinary manner, though one that unwittingly revealed his high appreciation of his associate's reputation for profundity. Finney was conducting the preliminary exercises on a Sunday morning in which this professor was

---

[3]*Oberlin News*, August 20, 1874.

to preach, and he prayed, "That my brother might be baptized with the Spirit, and might have great simplicity of speech and clearness of utterance given him, so that the great truths of the gospel should be made plain and brought within our reach, so that we should not all have to get up on tiptoe to understand what he is saying."

As a pastor, Finney attended faithfully to the spiritual functions of his office. In addition to preaching, he led the weekly prayer meeting, held an inquiry meeting at some time during each week, and always stood ready to respond to every genuine call from those who were in spiritual trouble.

Appendix B

A Testimonial Letter

President Finney's Prayer for Rain
Washington, D.C., January 1, 1912
Professor George S. Ormsby
Xenia, Ohio

My Dear Sir:

I acknowledge with pleasure your letter of 21st last, in which you remind me of our meeting in this city some years ago and of our conversation of Oberlin and of the "mighty man of God" who was president of the college then. You recall a poor attempt I made then to describe the man, the conditions that called for the prayer he uttered, the striking climax of the instant event, and ask that I put in writing as much of the story as may yet remain in memory.

There is no memorandum within my reach by which I can with certainty give the exact date of the occurrence, but marshalling such general facts as remain in mind, which fix the milestones in my pilgrimage of near 76 years, I conclude that it was probably when I had reached my 16th year, or the summer of 1852.

From an early day in the springtime of the year the skies had withheld the rain; indeed, the curtain of the clouds was seldom drawn across the face of the sun. The summer was passing and eyes had become wearied with looking toward the heavens for relief. The meadows gave little hope of providing provender for the winter, the pastures were brown and bare, the corn was cut short in its growth; its leaves were curled and yellow as if to mock the passerby with visions of golden ears that would never reach the granary. The brooks had ceased to flow; their ponds had dried up. Many wells were near exhaustion. The call on them to share their contents with the domestic animals of the farm had often changed "the moss-covered bucket" into a dried out and leaking receptacle, which if sent down too often found no answer to its quest. If one ventured into the pasture-field, the grazing beasts ceased their search for food and followed one about as if asking pity and relief. In those days the farms had been but partially cleared of the giant trees that covered the earth's floor in all that region when pioneers of Oberlin College threaded their way to the spot where now stands the college campus, the stately buildings, and the dear old church where President Finney so long preached and prayed.

At the time of which I write, the wild things of the woods still found ample food and shelter on the borders of the cleared fields. The woods were alive with squirrels. The raccoon and the opossum still sheltered there. In this day of distress they forgot their fear of man and following the fences were found about the houses and out-buildings, and so heedless of the man and his dog that many of the squirrel kind were killed with sticks and stones in the hands of passing boys. The grasshopper adding its burden as of old was there in unwonted numbers, and the creeping things "whose day is the nighttime" came out with the sun to be trodden under foot of man. The face of the earth was seamed with cracks; its mouths were open for refreshing. I have given you this partial recital of conditions that you may better understand allusions in the prayer, some of which I recall, and will set down.

At the time I am writing of, I was a boy farmhand, living and laboring a little less than two miles from the Old Church at Oberlin. The Sunday school assembled within its walls at nine o'clock in the morning. I was a regular attendant. As I wended my dusty way toward the church that Lord's Day morning, there was no sign of relenting in the skies. "The heavens were as brass." The school dismissed, the congregation began to gather for the morning service. The organ welcomed them. There was a great choir gathered about it. The seats were well filled. There were hundreds of earnest people facing the pulpit when Professor Morgan—dear old John Morgan—whose ever-present smile was a benediction, mounted its steps. Then followed President Finney, a man of noble mold in both face and figure. He was in the fullness of his powers, and was, as many then thought and I still think, the greatest preacher of his day. The sun was shining. His house was only a short distance away, but he carried an umbrella to his seat. There were smiles, I am sure, at this. I know of one who smiled at the seeming unequal challenge of the Providence that ruled the hour. The service proceeded in order. The opening prayer was uttered by Professor Morgan, then came the voice of song; and when it died away, the president took his place to confess the sins of the people, to voice their distress, and to plead for mercy. There was great charm in this man. Nature set before her most skillful artificers the task of molding his form; His voice had the heart-melody of a mother when calling an erring child to a better way. His vision sometimes seemed to catch the dawning of "the day of days"; the oncoming to the judgment of all whose feet had ever trod the earth. In such moments standing in the midst of the platform pulpit, his foot advanced, his head thrown back, he looked in attitude and demeanor a Jupiter not dispensing the rains nor guiding the thunderbolts, but heaven's chief herald ordering the trumpet blast that should rend the hiding places of all the living and all the dead, one could fancy he heard an echo of the voice of the prophet of Galilee saying, "Our Father"—and so that day he spoke with the Father.

First, as always, remembering the great body of students sitting before him, he commended them to heaven's care, and especially that their feet might never stray from the straight and narrow path. Then giving liberty of speech to the chief burden of the hour, he spoke of the cloudless sun, of inanimate nature, instead of her summer garb of glory, wearing the garments of woe; of leaves shriveled and falling; that no flower reflected the smile of the Eternal to give his children joy, that the night was a glad shelter from a sun whose rising gave no promise of good but whose darkening shadows gave merciful relief to eyes weary of looking on "the abomination of desolation." Then he spoke with the Father of living things, the work of His own hands. How the wild things of the woods, forgetting their fear of man, sought His habitation; that the creeping things whose day is night wandered abroad in the morning to be trodden under foot of man and beast. He told the *All Merciful* of the cattle wandering over fields "that yielded no meat," looking reproachfully into men's faces as if to inquire for what sin of theirs they were so sorely afflicted, and voicing the universal cry of things animate and inanimate, his cheeks moistened with tears, he exclaimed, "Even the thirsty earth opens its mouth wide and cries to God for water!" He told of the prophet's joy, when the cloud no greater than a man's hand challenged the sun, and with filial confidence bespoke the coming blessing.

The Amen had not ceased its echo, the suppliant still stood at the desk, when with a crash and a roar resounding from the roof of the great church, a flood of rain descended. In broken accents he said, "The Lord heard while we were yet speaking." And the choir, with every voice in the congregation attuned to song, burst forth with Luther's glad anthem "Praise God from whom all blessings flow."

In later years I have now and then related this incident of the long ago to ears, some in a receptive and some in a critical mood. The younger auditors no doubt wondered how so much of the memory could remain after the lapse of many years, and some inclined to raise a query about miracle and special providence.

Perhaps in those days the Christian peoples dwelt too much on a "wrestling Jacob." Perchance in these later years our vision is so occupied with the "eternal plan" that we lose touch with the *Father's hand*. However this may be, you and I, who are upon the borderline, know how vividly old-time memories come to those who sit in the lengthening shadows of the present, and how pleasant to us are all the gleams of the past that speak of God's goodness, though dispensed with a chastening hand.

Wishing you all happiness in this New Year.

Faithfully yours,
S. S. Burdett

Appendix C

Charles Grandison Finney
A Biographical Sketch

The son of a Revolutionary War veteran, Charles G. Finney was born on August 29, 1792, in Warren, Connecticut. His lack of religious education and upbringing was a result of the general decline of Christian and biblical teaching in America following the war. True, there were times of revival in the early 1800s, but Finney was not raised in a Christian home, and he never heard a prayer in his father's house. His father did become a Christian after Finney, as an adult, presented the Gospel to him.

Finney was highly gifted intellectually, culturally, and physically. Mostly self-educated, he became a schoolteacher, and at the age of twenty-six, he became an apprentice in the law office of Benjamin Wright in Adams, New York. He had been told that he could study law independently and pass the bar exam in two years, half the time that it would take to attend Yale.

While studying for his bar exam, and during his preparation for court cases, Finney discovered that the foundation for American law was the Bible, that American law appealed to the Bible as its absolute standard for law. So he bought his first Bible to help him study law. He meticulously looked up each biblical reference in his law books to study it in its proper biblical context. This study of the law on the one hand and of the Bible on the other convinced him that the Bible was indeed God's Word. He was weighed in the balance, and knew that he needed to attend to the state of his soul, to either go to Christ for salvation or continue living a worldly and selfish life deserving of God's judgment.

Finney was known in Adams as a despiser of religion, even though he used his considerable musical talent to direct the young people's choir at church. He sometimes attended prayer meeting, but his pastor told the church he despaired of Finney's conversion. Nevertheless, the Word and the Spirit of God were doing their work, and on October 10, 1821, Finney gave his life willingly and completely to Jesus Christ, taking Him as Lord and Savior, resolving to leave the practice of law to plead Christ's cause.

Finney's theological understanding grew rapidly through his reading of the Bible, much prayer, and heated discussions with his hyper-Calvinist pastor, George Gale, a Princeton graduate. Gale and Finney engaged in heavy theological debates, and Gale finally adopted Finney's views, though some years later.

Charles Finney was licensed to preach on December 30, 1823, at the age of thirty-one, and became a Presbyterian missionary, traveling throughout the Western District of New York. Revivals immediately accompanied his preaching. Having been trained for the bar, he preached for a verdict as he took God's side against the sinner, expecting people to repent of their sins and come out on the Lord's side *immediately*. He preached the justice of God in love, explained the purpose of the Atonement, and many from all classes of society became Christians.

In 1824 he married Lydia Andrews, but shortly after their marriage revival broke out as a result of his preaching and they had to be separated for six months. Lydia died in 1847. He then married a widow, Elizabeth F. Atkinson, a woman who provided much help in his revivals, but she died in 1863. His third wife, Rebecca Rayl, survived him, living to 1907.

Finney's success in promoting revivals prompted him to give a series of lectures that later became the famous book *Lectures on Revivals of Religion*. This book has sold in the millions; remaining in print for more than one hundred and fifty years, and having been translated into many languages. These lectures and his *Autobiography* have inspired revivals around the world. When his *Lectures on Revivals of Religion* were published in England, revivals broke out almost immediately at the application of his principles. English churchmen convinced him to make two revival tours of the United Kingdom, and here he saw the same success he had seen in America. It is reported that in 1905–06, a book detailing his revivals and revival methods inspired a great revival in China.

Finney's principles can have the same result today when, in obedience to the Holy Spirit, people read and apply the biblical truths Finney discovered and revealed in a new, challenging way. As one old Norwegian evangelist always advised, "To keep the revival fires burning in your heart, read from the book of Acts and from Charles Finney every day."

One of Finney's most famous revivals was in Rochester, New York, in 1830. Of that revival, the great preacher Lyman Beecher said, "That was the greatest work of God and the greatest revival of religion that the world has ever seen in so short a time. One hundred thousand were reported to have connected themselves with churches as the result of that great revival. This is unparalleled in the history of the church and of the progress of religion." Beecher had at one time opposed Finney's work, saying, "You mean to come into Connecticut and carry a streak of fire to Boston. But if you attempt it, as the Lord lives, I'll meet you at the state line and call out the artillerymen and fight every inch of the way to Boston, and I'll fight you there." Later, Finney and Beecher worked closely together for a revival in Boston, and he was to compare Finney favorably with one of their contemporaries, Asahel Nettleton, saying, "Nettleton 'sets snares' for sinners, but Finney rode them down with a cavalry charge."

In addition to his revival labors, Finney held three pastorates. In 1833 he pastored the Chatham Street Chapel in New York City. In 1835 he divided his time between teaching at Oberlin College, Oberlin, Ohio (a school he helped to found), and serving as pastor of the Broadway Tabernacle in New York City (a building he helped design). He became pastor of the Oberlin Congregational Church in 1837, a position he held for the next thirty-five years.

Finney became famous for his revivals while still a young man, and later he became a noted systematic theologian. Results of his preaching prove his theology worked. People became Christians when they heard him preach, and records indicate 85 percent of his converts remained true to their profession of faith. Likewise, thousands have since studied and applied his theology in their own ministry with similar results, whether they were evangelists, preachers, pastors, or laypeople seeking to obey God's call to evangelize the world.

His lectures on theology are found in his two books *The Heart of Truth* and *Finney's Systematic Theology*, both published by Bethany House. (*The Heart of Truth* is currently out of print.)

Reading the collections of Finney's sermons on Romans in *Principles of Victory* and *Principles of Liberty* is the best introduction to his thought on both biblical and theological subjects. Most of Finney's early followers learned of him first through his sermons, and then were mentally and spiritually prepared to grapple with his systematic theology. This can be our approach today.

On a more personal note, my theological education had so educated me away from common sense that I could not understand his *Systematic Theology* when I first began to read it. It was not until I had read many of his sermons and had the help of the Holy Spirit in prayer that the light shined. And the labor of studying Finney's theology was well worth the cost. The editor of one English edition of Finney's *Lectures on Systematic Theology* wrote, "The Editor frankly confesses that when a student he would gladly have bartered half the books in his library to have gained a single perusal of these lectures; and he cannot refrain from expressing the belief that no young student of theology will ever regret the purchase or perusal of Mr. Finney's lectures." For a more thorough understanding of the power of Finney's theology, see my introduction to *Finney's Systematic Theology* (the complete and newly expanded 1878 edition) published by Bethany House Publishers, 1994, xiii–xxvi.

Prayer was one of the most important reasons for Finney's success. He did everything in a spirit of prayer. He prayed for divine guidance in reading the Scriptures, preaching, teaching, writing, his work as an evangelist, and even his praying. While Finney was lecturing to students at Oberlin College, a student once asked him a question about a passage in the Bible. Finney confessed he did not know the answer, immediately knelt down in prayer before the class, and soon rose with a glowing face to give the answer the Lord had shown him. Some classes became actual prayer meetings, when the class subject was sometimes set aside to attend to the spiritual state of the students. At other times he would go to a student's room for a time of private prayer with the student.

Finney served as president of Oberlin College from 1851–66. His presence at the college from its beginning insured its success, as students wanted to come and learn from Mr. Finney how to do the work of an evangelist. He had insisted that blacks and women be admitted to the college on an equal basis when it was founded, and Oberlin became the first coeducational college in America. His popularity was still strong in 1851, for in his first year as president enrollment skyrocketed from 571 to 1,070 students.

Finney was strong and vigorous to the end of his life. He resigned his pastorate shortly before his death, but continued to preach and teach on occasion until he died from a heart attack on August 16, 1875.

I became a Bible-believing Christian after I read some of Charles G. Finney's books, and found in them the answers to certain theological questions that had plagued me. At this same time I had been studying the works of the late Francis A. Schaeffer, whose writings answered certain crucial philosophical questions. I owe my salvation to a loving God, who sent His Son to save me from sin, and who sent His Holy Spirit to guide me into the truth of His Word. And I thank God for the writings of Charles Finney and Francis Schaeffer. I believe both men were called by God to be men of their time, that each man became the greatest proponent of evangelical Christianity in his own century, and that the works of both will have lasting significance, saving many lives.

People such as the late Gordon Olson and the late Harry Conn spent a lifetime researching Finney's ideas and making these available to others in a significant and contemporary way. Organizations such as Bethany Fellowship (with its college of missions and Bethany House Publishers), Bible Research Fellowship, and Men for Missions have remained strong as they have adhered to the biblical and theological principles of Charles Finney, and as they have applied them in practical ways. Francis and Edith Schaeffer's work will continue through their books and those written about their life. (See my books, *Francis and Edith Schaeffer* (Minneapolis: Bethany House Publishers, 1996) and *How God Teaches Us to Pray: Lessons From the Lives of Francis and Edith Schaeffer* [Milton Keynes, England: Nelson Word, Ltd., 1993, currently out of print].)

If we will take the time *to study* both Charles Finney and Francis Schaeffer, *and apply* what we learn from them (as they each correct the other in our thinking), then we will develop our understanding of the Christian gospel in such fullness that the Holy Spirit will bless our endeavors for the kingdom of God and for the salvation of souls.

As we study the Bible and theology in preparation for our ministry, whether we are clergy or laypeople, let us not push aside the centrality of prayer in maintaining our relationship with God. Finney warns us all:

> I am convinced that nothing in the whole Christian religion is so difficult, and so rarely attained, as a praying heart. Without this you are as weak as weakness itself. If you lose your spirit of prayer, you will do nothing, or next to nothing, though you had the intellectual endowment of an angel. If you lose your spirituality, you had better stop and break off in the midst of your preparations, and repent and turn to God, or go about some other employment, for I cannot contemplate a more loathsome and abominable object than an earthly-minded minister. The blessed Lord deliver and preserve His dear church from the guidance and influence of men who know not what it is to pray.

Love in the Lamb,
L. G. Parkhurst, Jr.